TECHNOLOGY, COMPUTERS, AND THE SPECIAL NEEDS LEARNER

TECHNOLOGY, COMPUTERS, AND THE SPECIAL NEEDS LEARNER

John R. Ray
M. Kathleen Warden

University of Tennessee-Knoxville

DELMAR PUBLISHERS

I(T)P

NOTICE TO THE READER

Cover: David Prusko

Delmar Staff
Publisher: David C. Gordon
Associate Editor: Erin J. O'Connor
Project Editor: Colleen A. Corrice

Production Coordinator: James Zayicek
Art/Design Coordinator: Timothy J. Conners

Copyright © 1995
By Delmar Publishers
a division of International Thomson Publishing Inc.

The ITP logo is a trademark under license.

Printed in the United States of America

For more information, contact:

Delmar Publishers
3 Columbia Circle, Box 15015
Albany, New York 12212-5015

International Thomson Publishing Europe
Berkshire House 168–173
High Holborn
London WCIV7AA
England

Thomas Nelson Australia
102 Dodds Street
South Melbourne, 3205
Victoria, Australia

Nelson Canada
1120 Birchmount Road
Scarborough, Ontario
Canada M1K 5G4

International Thomson Editores
Campos Eliseos 385, Piso 7
Col Polanco
11560 Mexico D F Mexico

International Thomson Publishing GmbH
Königswinterer Strasse 418
53227 Bonn
Germany

International Thomson Publishing Asia
221 Henderson Road
#05–10 Henderson Building
Singapore 0315

International Thomson Publishing–Japan
Hirakawacho Kyowa Builing, 3F
2-2-1 Hirakawacho
Chiyoda-ku, Tokyo 102
Japan

1 2 3 4 5 6 7 8 9 10 XXX 01 00 99 98 97 96 95 94

Library of Congress Cataloging-in-Publication Data

Ray, John R.
    Technology, computers, and the special needs learner / John R.
Ray, M. Kathleen Warden.
    —1st ed.
      p.   cm.
    Includes bibliographical references and index.
    ISBN 0-8273-6476-8
    1. Special education—United States—Computer-assisted instruction.   2. Educational
technology—United States.   I. Warden, M. Kathleen.   II. Title.
LC3969.5.R39   1994
371.9′043—dc20   94-6812
                                                                 CIP

Contents

Dedication

For my wife, Nancy
For my soulmate, Peter

Acknowledgments

The authors and staff at Delmar Publishers wish to express their appreciation to the reviewers of this manuscript who made thoughtful and constructive suggestions.

Linda Heenan
Board of Cooperative Educational Services
Albany, NY

Cynthia M. King
Gallaudet University
Washington, DC

David Dean Richey
Tennessee Technological University
Cookeville, TN

Katherine K. Sheng
The City College, CUNY
New York City, NY

PREFACE

Technology, Computers, and the Special Needs Learner grew out of our belief that teachers and preservice education students need a book that gives special attention to this topic. Teachers are concerned about how to serve all of their students. This we know. What we provide is information to teachers that will encourage and teach them to be informed consumers of technology—specifically where special education students are concerned.

The technology we describe is developed for administrators, teachers, and special needs students. Technology users should keep in mind, however, that parents and non-special education students may also benefit from some of this technology. For example, there are students in classrooms who are *not* designated in need of special education services, but who nevertheless, seem to lag behind age-mates. Certainly these students could benefit from software that supports reading, math, or written composition. Parents may also benefit. If they serve as volunteers in the schools, use them in expanding computer work with all students. Parents could enhance their own learning, and/or suggest novel ways to use the technology. They also learn to be effective advocates for expanded opportunities for both special needs learners and other learners.

With regard to special needs students, the text specifically focuses on learner characteristics rather than disability label. Disability labels provide little information about students' educational needs.

This book is more than a how-to manual. Rather, it is designed to help the teacher or teacher education student teach from a perspective that embraces technology in the classroom as a way to enrich everyone's (teacher's, parent's, administrator's, student's) lives.

The book also strongly supports the position that "You Ain't Seen Nothing Yet." The growth curve for usage is starting up. Granted, scarce resources, little time, and a history of apathy are obstacles. However, the legislation is in place, the quality and quantity of hardware and software increase daily, and the "feel" for change is rampant.

We believe the future is bright and that instructional services are destined for rapid improvement. This book represents a beginning in the evolution of these efforts.

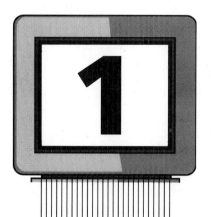

The Promise, The Hope, and The Reality

Objectives

After reading this chapter, you should be able to:

- Describe the objectives of Public Law (PL) 94-142 and PL 101-476.
- Define mainstreaming.
- Define the seven special education disability groups.
- Discuss classroom accommodations for each disability group.
- Discuss general software characteristics needed for each disability group.
- Distinguish between acceptable and offensive language when referring to people with disabilities.

The Promise

In 1975 the U.S. Congress passed Public Law 94-142, The Education for All Handicapped Children Act, also known as the mainstreaming law. PL 94-142 guarantees that all children with disabilities have a right to a "free, appropriate, public education in the most appropriate, least restrictive environment (LRE)." More important, the law means that a child with a disability cannot be denied education in a public school based solely on his or her disability. The promise was that whenever possible and appropriate a child with a disabling condition would be educated in a local public school with age-mates rather than in an institution or a program solely for students with disabilities. The law also stipulates that parents must be active partners in devising an education plan for their child. In tandem with appropriate school system and/or medical personnel, parents meet and devise a written plan—an Individualized Education Program (IEP)—that will be carried out by the school. Figure 1-1 shows the percentage of all students with disabilities served in six educational placements.

In 1990 Congress passed PL 101-476, Individuals with Disabilities Education Act (IDEA), an updated version of PL 94-142. Just prior to the passage of PL

Figure 1-1
Percentage of all students with disabilities age 3–21 served in six educational placements.

Note: Includes data from 50 states, the District of Columbia, and Puerto Rico. Separate school includes both public and private separate school facilities. Residential includes both public and private residential facilities. *Courtesy of: U.S. Department of Education, Office of Special Education Programs. Data Analysis System (DANS). (1991)*

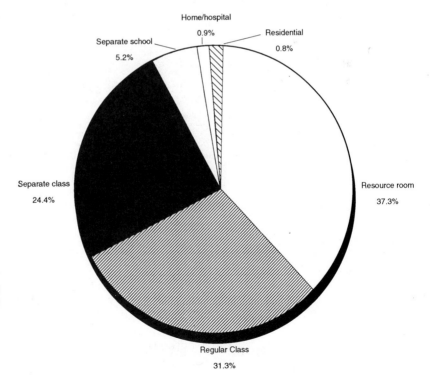

Home/hospital
0.9%

Residential
0.8%

Separate school
5.2%

Separate class
24.4%

Resource room
37.3%

Regular Class
31.3%

101-476, the Office of Special Education Programs (OSEP) issued a policy letter stating that if participants on an IEP team determine a child requires assistive technology as part of special education or a related service, then the services must be provided at no cost to the parents. Subsequently PL 101-476 defined assistive technology device and assistive technology service. In general, an assistive device is any item that is used to increase, maintain, or improve functional capabilities of individuals with disabilities. An assistive technology service is any service that directly assists a person with a disability in the selection, acquisition, or use of an assistive technology device. Figure 1-2 shows a summary of the definitions of assistive technology and service mandated by PL 101-476. In Figure 1-3, U.S. Senator Tom Harkin (whose brother is deaf) describes why he sponsored PL 100-407, Technology-Related Assistance for Individuals with Disabilities Act (1988), an act that is part of the mandated rights to technology assistance for persons with disabilities.

Figure 1-2
PL 101-476,
Individuals with
Disabilities Education
Act (IDEA).

- Defines assistive technology device to mean any item, piece of equipment, or product, whether acquired commercially off the shelf, modified, or customized, which is used to increase, maintain, or improve functional capabilities of individuals with disabilities (same definition as is used in PL 100-407, Technology-Related Assistance for Individuals with Disabilities Act [1988]).

- Defines assistive technology service to mean any service that directly assists an individual with a disability in the selection, acquisition, or use of an assistive technology device. Such term includes:

   A. The evaluation of the needs of an individual with disability, including a functional evaluation of the individual in the individual's customary environment

   B. Purchasing, leasing, or otherwise providing for the acquisition of assistive technology devices by individuals with disabilities

   C. Selecting, designing, fitting, customizing, adapting, applying, maintaining, repairing, or replacing of assistive technology devices

   D. Coordinating and using other therapies, intervention, or services with assistive technology devices, such as those associated with existing education and rehabilitation places and programs

   E. Training or technical assistance for an individual with disabilities, or, where appropriate, the family of an individual with disabilities

   F. Training or technical assistance for professionals (including individuals providing education and rehabilitation services), employers, or other individuals who provide services to, employ, or are otherwise substantially involved in the major life functions of individuals with disabilities.

I know a young girl, 11 years old, who is severely impaired by cerebral palsy and mental retardation. Hers was an isolated childhood. She could not play as other children do. And she was unable to communicate at all until the University Affiliated Program at the University of Iowa offered her a childhood through the use of customized devices. Today she communicates by using a headmounted light pointer the university program developed for her; she points the light at pictures on a board. With the help of another device the university developed using microswitches that require minimal hand movement, she also plays with battery-operated toys.

Astrophysicist Stephen Hawking suffers from Lou Gehrig's disease (ALS) and cannot talk or write. Assistive technology has allowed him to write a best-selling book and to lecture internationally. But most importantly to the world, it allows him to continue his work and contribute to scientific knowledge.

Just as it did for the girl in Iowa and for Hawking, adaptive technology can make a tremendous difference in the lives of all of us. Disabilities confront everyone in varying degrees. As we age, more and more of us may find ourselves or someone we know facing a disability. It is estimated that nearly two-thirds of America's population will one day suffer partial or total hearing loss. Glaucoma and cataracts threaten our vision as we grow older. Stroke victims may find themselves unable to communicate and function independently; others are rendered immobile by falls and accidents.

Optacon, VersaBraille, speech synthesizers, voice communication boards, and the emerging brain-/computer interface are just a few products on the growing list of devices that are breaking down barriers for the disabled.

Last year, as chairman of the Senate Subcommittee on the Handicapped, I introduced a bill called the Technology-Related Assistance for Individuals with Disabilities Act of 1988. Following two days of testimony on how technology has already helped the disabled to lead productive lives, it became clear that America needs a comprehensive, responsive, and coordinated system to stimulate new developments and make them accessible and affordable to disabled people.

The act, which was approved by both houses and signed by President Reagan in just two months, was designed to do just what its name suggests. It established a federal program through which states receive money to conduct research in assistive technologies, disseminate information on those technologies, and offer assistance to the disabled to obtain them.

Rarely had a bill received the kind of support from both sides of the aisle and from consumer and professional groups that this one did. Obviously, many people believe in the promise that technology brings to the lives of people with disabilities. And they welcome the help of the federal government in turning that promise into reality.

Support for that vision continued into this year when the Bush administration recommended more than doubling funds to implement the bill. The appropriation, which will increase from $5,000,000 to nearly $11,000,000, is the largest percentage increase in a domestic program. But while we have made real progress in the past several years, far more needs to be done.

Today, the federal government funds hundreds of millions of dollars in unemployment disability payments to persons who could be employed if they had access to assistive technology. Investments in technology to keep people working can save taxpayers and employers much of the cost of long-term disability payments.

As a nation dedicated

(continued)

Figure 1-3
(*Continued*)

to freedom, indepen-dence, and the dignity of all human beings, it is the responsibility of all of us to look at disabled people and see what they can do, not what they can't. As-sistive technology gives us	a very powerful means to support the "can dos."— Tom Harkin ——————————— Tom Harkin (D-Iowa), whose brother is deaf, is the only United States sen-	ator proficient in sign lan-guage. He is chairman of the Senate Subcommittee on the Handicapped and of the Subcommittee on Appropriations for Labor, Health and Human Ser-vices, and Education.

Source: *PC Computing*, (1989, July), *2* (7), p. 91.

Thus, the promise offered by these laws (PL 94-142 and PL 101-476) was to educate children with disabling conditions in as "normal" a situation as was appropriate and to provide any assistive devices necessary to enhance the educa-tional experience. (See Appendix A for selected litigation and legislation affecting special education.)

The Hope

Educators hoped that by normalizing the educational experience of children with disabilities (this movement by the mid-1980s was called the Regular Education Initiative) that these children would have a higher probability of not being handicapped by their disabilities. The children would have interaction with non-disabled peers; they would have the same daily experiences, good or bad, from going on field trips to attending school sporting events, from dealing with lunch-room chaos to resolving conflicts on the playground with their age-mates. Profes-sionals hoped these learning experiences would enrich the lives of children with disabilities just as they enrich the lives of all children. Another hope was that exposure to a regular curriculum would give children with disabilities the chance to learn things that special educators perhaps assumed they could not learn. For example, the label *handicapped* or *disabled*, dictated that somehow a given child must be limited; therefore, the curriculum for that child had to be limited as well. More and more educators and learning theorists began to realize that learning is a multisource phenomenon (Iran-Nejad, McKeachie, & Berliner, 1990) and that simple stimulus-response work is only one part of education. So the idea was to enrich the context in which children operated to promote more learning.

The assumption was that a public school classroom provides a greater variety of experiences than a special education classroom. Further, educators hoped to enrich the regular classroom by the very presence of children who were different. In a pluralistic society, school was viewed as the place to learn that diversity is a positive thing. People all have things to teach each other, and educators thought diversity could be best learned through interaction. For example, if a "non-disabled" child went to school with a child who used a wheelchair, and each experienced the other as an average person, it would be likely that when they reached adulthood what would matter would be a person's ability to do the job—not the fact that one uses a wheelchair and the other doesn't.

Another hope was that teachers faced with the diversity created by differences among children would find their creativity stretched. In coming up with novel ways to deal with students who require extraordinary teaching methods, both teachers and students would benefit.

The Reality

On the whole mainstreaming has been a benefit for students with disabilities (Algozzine, Maheady, Sacca, O'Shea, & O'Shea, 1990; Grangreco, Dennis, Cloninger, Edelman, & Schattman, 1993; Truesdell & Abramson, 1992; Wang & Walberg, 1988; York, Vandercook, MacDonald, Heise-Neff, & Caughey, 1992; Zigmond & Baker, 1990). Many of the promises have been kept. But, as with any new system, there are problems. Educating children with disabilities with their nondisabled peers has benefits for both groups. The difficulty arises when children end up only being mainstreamed for lunch and recess. A placement like this meets the letter of the law, but hardly meets its spirit. There are cases, however—and this is crucially important—in which this kind of mainstreaming is appropriate. What is inappropriate is this type of placement when it has occurred only to meet the convenience of the school and not the needs of the child with a disability.

Another reality is that teachers are often forced to deal with large classes and few resources. Adding a child with a disability to the class without the necessary support services can overload even the most creative teachers. Hence, placement decisions are crucial. The phrase "most appropriate, least restrictive environment" must carry great weight. It could be argued that if children are placed in a classroom where they cannot do the academic work, then the placement is inappropriate, no matter how appropriate the peer interaction may be. On the other hand, if the major goal is to work on the child's social skills with peers and the academic work is secondary, then the class may be an appropriate placement.

Another reality is that parents' rights can be overlooked. It is not unusual for an IEP meeting to be scheduled. The school personnel arrive at the meeting with the IEP already written. It is then presented to the parents as a completed item. According to the law, parents are to take part in the writing of the IEP, not just sign a document that is presented to them. Fortunately, many school systems are very conscientious about making certain that parents understand their rights and obligations in their child's education.

Finally, the writers of PL 94-142 and the supporters of the law worked under the assumption that all children with disabilities would have a better educational experience in a nonresidential school. The idea was that all institutional placements promoted segregation and were inherently unequal. In some situations this is not the case (Byrnes, 1990). Suppose a child who is profoundly deaf has undergone extensive auditory and speech training. The child is found to excel in language development and acquisition of world knowledge only when sign language is the mode of communication. This child is in the first grade with a sign language interpreter. Unfortunately, the only person this child communicates with is the interpreter. The child is socially isolated. There is no interaction on the playground, in the cafeteria, or in class, except with the teacher through the interpreter. There is no after-school play because the children cannot communicate with each other. Academically this child may be making appropriate progress, but life is lonely. Would it not be appropriate for this child to be in a residential school for the deaf—if possible, as a day student? At most schools for the deaf everyone uses sign language. The child is no longer isolated. This is not an easy decision to make. But this example shows that educational placement for all children is a complicated, multifaceted proposition.

Another example is of a child who is severely physically disabled. This child could be placed in an institution with a pool for physical therapy, a physical therapist who can work with the child every day, an occupational therapist, a speech therapist, a specialist in prosthetic and assistive devices, and a regular school curriculum. This child also could be placed in a regular school with none of these special services. What is the most appropriate placement? How do we prioritize physical needs and social needs? What is the long-term prognosis? Would placement in an institutional setting for a few years allow this child to progress to the point where public school could be a better experience at a later time?

We offer this explanation of the laws and the comments on the promise, the hope, and the reality to give a flavor of how complicated and confusing decisions about children with special needs can be. There is no one formula that will work for these children, just as there is no one formula that will work for every child. In this book we will present ways to enhance learning for students with special needs using computers in the classroom. We are operating on several assumptions:

1. We will focus on special education students who are in regular classrooms. (Certainly, however, we hope any suggestions we offer could be applied in any classroom.)

2. We are assuming that students in the classrooms have been appropriately placed.
3. We are assuming that the class is taught by an excellent teacher. Technology will never substitute for poor teaching. Nor will technology make a poor teacher better.
4. We believe that computer technology wisely used can enhance a student's strengths and shore up weaknesses. We assume that teachers will want to build on students' strengths.
5. We will categorize students according to disabling condition only to provide a frame of reference for the reader. Categories like learning disabled, visually impaired, physically disabled, and the like, give no information on how to teach students so labeled. We will offer suggestions on appropriate software and hardware for specific learner objectives or for ways to compensate for specific learner characteristics that handicap the student.
6. Finally, we will not focus on the classification level (mild, moderate, severe, or profound) of the disabling condition. Ultimately, classifications may not be useful. What matters is how the student functions. For example, a student who is severely visually impaired may be able to read large print. The only accommodation needed may be a device that enlarges the print from a book or from typed text on a computer screen. A child who is profoundly deaf may function as if there is a mild hearing loss. The student may be an excellent speech reader, and may need no accommodation other than a relatively quiet room so a hearing aid can help and to have people face the student while speaking. By the same token, children who have been classified as mildly impaired may function as if they have severe to profound impairments.

We emphasize again that many accommodations recommended here should enhance the learning of all students in the classroom—not just students who are labeled "disabled." Technology specifically can be used to facilitate all types of learning activities—from individual review, drill, and practice, to cooperative learning situations. Technology in the classroom should improve the quality of life for students and teachers.

An Introduction to Special Needs Learners

There is a difference between a disability and a handicap. A disability is the actual presence of a physical or psychological problem that may or may not result in a handicap for a person. For example, a person who is deaf is handicapped in the use of a telephone (unless there is access to a telecommunication device for the deaf [TDD]), but a person who is blind is not handicapped if he or she wishes to talk on a phone (only dialing presents a problem). Ultimately, how handicapped a person is depends on environmental conditions. It is one of the purposes of this book to demonstrate how computer use can reduce the probability that a student with a disability will experience the classroom as a place where a disability turns into a handicap. One of the ways to lessen the probability that a student with a disability will be viewed as a "lesser" person is to be careful of the language we use. Language has power. What may appear to be prejudice may only be an insensitive or careless use of language when referring to persons with disabilities. For guidelines for acceptable and sensitive use of language, see Figures 1-5 and 1-6.

We are assuming that you will be encountering students who have been identified as having a disability and who have an IEP in place. It is not our purpose to describe how to diagnose a disability. Should you suspect that a student has problems with learning due to a disability, you should meet with a supervisor and follow the school system's guidelines for referring that child for assessment.

The following section will describe students according to disability category. PL 94-142 lists specific handicapping conditions. Students must be designated as fitting a category before they can receive special education services.

Figure 1-4
Student and teacher using a program that displays speech on a graph. *Courtesy of International Business Machines Corporation.*

Figure 1-7 shows the percent of total enrollment in federally funded programs for students with disabilities from 1977 to 1989. These figures provide useful information to professionals for planning such varied instructional activites, interventions, and hardware/software acquisitions.

Figure 1-5
Guidelines for sensitive use of language.

1. Do not refer to a disability unless it is relevant.
2. Do not sensationalize a disability by saying "a victim of," "afflicted with," and so on. Instead, say "person who has multiple sclerosis" or "people who have had polio."
3. Avoid emotional descriptions. Say "uses a wheelchair" rather than "confined to a wheelchair"; "walks with crutches" rather than "is crippled."
4. Avoid labeling and grouping people, as in "the disabled," "the deaf," "a paraplegic." Instead, say "people with disabilities," "people who are deaf," "a man who has paraplegia." (Note that the words "disabled," "blind," and "deaf" are adjectives, not nouns!)
5. Avoid portraying people with disabilities who succeed as remarkable or superhuman. This implies that it is unusual for people with disabilities to have talents or skills.
6. Avoid using the word "handicapped" in regard to a disability, as in "handicapped entrance" or "handicapped transportation." Instead, say "*accessible* entrance." The word "handicapped" serves to segregate rather than integrate people with disabilities.
7. Avoid putting disability issues into a medical context. The overwhelming majority of people with disabilities are not sick. Words like "patient," "case," and "invalid" should not be used. Most current disability issues concern civil rights, education, or accessibility.
8. Do not assume that a person with a speech impediment or mobility impairments has some form of mental limitation.
9. Avoid an overfamiliar tone in referring to people with disabilities. A person with a disability deserves the same courtesy of address and reference as a person without a disability.
10. If you wish to speak to a person with a disability, address him or her directly, rather than addressing someone who is with that person.
11. Remember that people with mental retardation often are quite articulate. Others may understand more than they are able to communicate.

Adapted from a publication by the Coalition for Tennesseans with Disabilities, 2416 Twenty-first Avenue South, Suite 206, Nashville, TN 37212.

Figure 1-6
Examples of
acceptable and
offensive language.

Acceptable	Offensive
disabled	crippled, deformed
nondisabled	able-bodied, normal, healthy
people with disabilities persons with disabilities	the disabled the handicapped
uses a wheelchair is a wheelchair user	is confined to a wheelchair is wheelchair bound
has cerebral palsy	is a cerebral palsy
has had polio	suffers from polio
has a specific learning disability	is learning disabled
has a speech disability	is speech impaired
people who are blind, visually impaired, deaf, or hearing impaired	the blind, the visually impaired, the deaf, or the hearing impaired, deaf-mutes, deaf dumb
person with mental illness	the mentally ill crazy person, psycho
person with mental retardation, developmental delay, or developmental disability	the mentally retarded, mentally deficient, or feeble- minded a retard or retardate
person with Down syndrome	the Down syndrome child, Mongoloid (Never!)
people who have epilepsy	epileptics

(*continued*)

Acceptable	Offensive
seizures	fits
congenital disability	birth defect

This brochure was produced at Vanderbilt University by the Equal Access Committee. It is based, in part, on "Guidelines for Reporting and Writing about People with Disabilities," a pamphlet published by the Research and Training Center on Independent Living, University of Kansas, 1984. Permission to reprint may be obtained by calling the Opportunity Development Center (615/322-4705 V/TDD).

Published by the Office of University Publications Design and Layout by the University Designer, 1988.

Adapted from a publication by the Coalition for Tennesseans with Disabilities, 2416 Twenty-first Avenue South, Suite 206, Nashville, TN 37212.

Figure 1-6 *(Continued)*

Figure 1-7
Percent of total enrollment in federally-supported programs for students with disabilities 1977–1989.

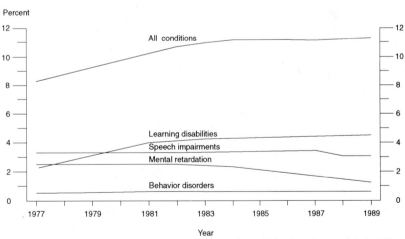

Source: U.S. Department of Education, Office of Special Education and Rehabilitative Services, National Longitudinal Transition Study, Youth with Disabilities During Transition: An Overview of Descriptive Findings from the National Longitudinal Transition Study, May, 1989; Annual Report to Congress on the Implementation of the Handicapped Act, various years.
The Conditions of Education, 1991, Vol. 1, NCES, USDOE NCES 53.

A Comment on Children Who Have Retardation, a Behavior Disorder, or a Learning Disability

Some special educators support the idea that special education should not resort to the "MR," "BD," and "LD" categories for classifying children because these categories overlap so much (Hallahan & Kauffman, 1977) or because they may not be educationally relevant (Gajar, 1980). For example, a student who has a behavior disorder may have had to deal with academic failure as the result of an undiagnosed learning disability. The student may look like a child with a behavior disorder. By the same token, a child with undiagnosed mental retardation may develop behavior problems because of repeated academic problems. Or, a child with a true behavior disorder may develop the characteristics of a specific learning disability such as an attention disorder.

Rationale for Clustering into Five Categories the Characteristics for Seven Special Education Disability Groupings

For the reasons explained above, we focus on learner characteristics rather than the disability label attached to the student. We will place emphasis on learner characteristics and functional levels, and use seven special education categories because federal law requires that students with disabilities be classified before they can receive special education services. Legal categories, however, do not provide information about how to teach these students. What is of help is a determination of where a student may lag behind his or her peer group *and* where the student shows strengths in cognitive development.

The computer companies that produce educational software have recognized the shortcomings of simply using disability labels like mental retardation or learning disabled. For clarity and ease of reference, these companies cluster technologies and software into five disability areas hearing; learning; mobility; speech or language; vision and then provide information on what technologies and software are available under their rubric. Persons seeking information may cross-reference. For example, a child with a hearing disability may also have problems with language. So one looks for information under both the hearing and speech or language categories.

A Comment

Educational programs should pay attention to student strengths. Allow students to demonstrate what they can do. Experiment. Ask students for suggestions on what helps them and what they enjoy. Listen as well as teach.

Additionally, equal access to educational opportunities is a value teachers should hold. It is impossible to legislate a value, but if teachers believe that all students should have the education they would want for their own children, this value will directly influence how committed teachers are to providing equality of opportunity.

Learners Who Have a Vision Impairment

Students who have a vision impairment fall into two categories: legally blind and low vision. A person who is legally blind has 20/200 vision in the best eye with best correction or a visual field of less than 20 degrees. If your vision is 20/200 it means that you must stand 20 feet from an object in order to see it; a person with normal vision could stand 200 feet from the object and still see it. The normal eye has a field of vision of 180 degrees. If you put your arms to your side, raise them to shoulder height, look straight in front of you, and wiggle your thumbs, you can see your thumbs even though you are looking straight ahead. This type of vision is called peripheral vision. A person with a restricted visual field of 20 degrees or less has a tiny spot out of which to see, unlike the normal field of 180 degrees, and this spot of vision can be anywhere within the 180 degree arc. A student with low vision has 20/70 vision in the best eye with the best correction. These are eligibility determinations and have little to do with learning modes.

DEFINITION: Vision Handicapped

In general, the term *vision handicapped* is used to describe all degrees of visual impairment—a continuum from severe visual impairment to total blindness. According to Barraga, "a visually handicapped child is one whose visual impairment interferes with his optimal learning and achievement, unless adaptations are made in the methods of presenting learning experiences, the nature of the materials used, and/or in the learning environment" (1983, p. 25).

Classroom Considerations/Accommodations. Students with vision impairments learn much the same way that other students do. Most of the accommodations required for these students are straightforward. What a teacher must have is a functional visual assessment that a vision teacher can do and that should be included in a student's file. A functional visual assessment will tell the teacher what a child can see, that is, how a child can use his or her vision to acquire information. For example, it is possible that a student who is legally blind can read print if the 20 percent field of vision is central vision. There are many assistive devices available for students who are visually impaired. Most devices are part of a computer station (for example, a magnifier that can be attached to a computer screen). Specific assistive devices will be described in Chapter 6.*

There are several ways a classroom can be made more accessible to a student with vision impairments. The first is lighting. A student may be able to read print in very strong light. Unfortunately, many classrooms do not have enough light or one section of the room has better lighting than another. The student can usually help the teacher make the necessary accommodations. A halogen lamp at the student's workstation may be a good solution. The student's computer screen may need to be against a dark background to put the screen into relief. Some students who are light sensitive need low light in order to see. Some students will be unable to see the chalkboard no matter where they are seated; let them choose their own seating as you would a student without a disability.

Teacher organization is crucial for students who need to hold a lot of information in short-term memory, as students with vision impairments do. The more organized a teacher is during a lesson as well as throughout the day, the more cues these students will have as to how to move from task to task as well as how to accomplish a specific task. Something as simple as knowing the day's schedule of events allows a student to place materials and books or disks in the order in which they will be used. This can save a lot of time for the student; there will be no need to sort through books or try to read the braille labels on everything. Figure 1-8 provides an example of one way computers expand the world for the visually impaired.

Above all else, the teacher should encourage the student to take responsibility for belongings and necessary equipment. Just as you expect other students to arrive at school with paper, pencil, and books, the student with a vision impairment should be able to organize a desk or work area so that what is needed for various tasks can be located. It is crucial that students not fall victim to learned helplessness. Part of being a competent person is being accountable.

Software Characteristics. Software will be needed that addresses the needs of each group. For example, software for use with a speech/language synthesizer

---

Disclaimer: Mention of specific products and companies that produce them is not an endorsement of the company or the product but rather an example of the types of devices described. There are many more companies that produce such devices—too numerous to name. By the time of this publication, many companies and products would be added to the list. The purpose of this section is to provide basic knowledge of adaptive technology, what is available, and some guidelines for its use. There is no one particular device that is "the best." It depends on the characteristics of the individual who will be utilizing this equipment and what that individual plans to accomplish with it.

Figure 1-8
Computers Expand
World for Visually
Impaired.

COMPUTERS EXPAND WORLD FOR VISUALLY IMPAIRED
Michael Silence

After flunking out, Michael Matvy got through college with the help of tape recorded books.

Matvy has dyslexia—a reading ability impairment that also affects his ability to write.

Now a psychologist with Knox County's [Tennessee] schools, he's starting to use computer technology with visually handicapped students.

That technology is available at the same 40-year-old institution in Oak Ridge that helped Matvy through college.

The Tennessee Unit of Recording for the Blind, one of 32 studios in the nation and the single one in Tennessee, this month added "electronic-text" or "E-text."

Among its capabilities, E-text allows a blind person to read a book by placing a disk in a computer, which in turn produces Braille on a reusable latex pad next to the computer.

A computer program operates pins beneath the latex pad to produce the Braille. The operator controls what the computer brings up on the pad through the use of a computer mouse.

Also, there are Braille printers and programs that produce a synthesized voice to "read" the material aloud.

The Oak Ridge studio is approaching 30,000 borrowers, two-thirds of whom have access to a computer, said Petty Kreig, studio director.

Recording for the Blind studios are located in 16 states, and the master tape library contains nearly 80,000 books and other documents. The replacement cost for that library is estimated at nearly $240 million.

Both the national organization and the local unit were started after World War II to help injured veterans continue their educations.

The local unit, with an annual budget of about $80,000, is operated entirely by private donations, with about 25 percent coming from the Lions of Tennessee.

The local unit can provide about 700 titles from the master library, but that continues to grow as tapes are converted to computer disks.

With E-text, Matvy can dictate a report on a student to his secretary and edit it by having the computer's synthesized voice read it.

He's just beginning to explore the multitude of applications. The bottom line, he said, is "as more texts become available in E-text, the more users there will be."

For more information on the services available and how to obtain the necessary computer equipment, call the Oak Ridge unit at (615) 482-3496, or write to Recording for the Blind, 205 Badger Road, Oak Ridge, TN 37830.

The Knoxville News-Sentinel, Sunday, June 28, 1992.

may have application for use with persons with other disabilities. Additionally, teachers and other professionals should note that general software packages probably have utility for the learner with special needs under the proper circumstances. Any software that deals with memory skills, organization, and task analysis skills will be helpful. There are software packages available that convert text to braille or voice and these will be covered in the Chapter 6, Assistive Devices.

Learners Who Have a Hearing Impairment

Students who are hearing impaired fall into two categories: deaf and hard-of-hearing. A person is deaf if he or she cannot use hearing to acquire language and speech even with the help of a hearing aid. A person is hard-of-hearing if a hearing aid helps that person acquire language and speech. There are different degrees of hearing loss (mild to profound) and different types of hearing loss (conductive, sensorineural, mixed), but a teacher's concern is with how a student functions in the classroom and how a student acquires information.

DEFINITION: Hearing Impairment

Frisina, in a definition of hearing impairment, describes the physical and educational dimensions of the handicap:

> A deaf person is one whose hearing is disabled to an extent . . . that precludes the understanding of speech through the ear alone, with or without the use of a hearing aid.

> A hard-of-hearing person is one whose hearing is disabled to an extent . . . that makes difficult, but does not preclude, the understanding of speech through the ear alone, with or without a hearing aid. (1974, p. 3)

Classroom Considerations/Accommodations. The problem faced by students who are perlingually deaf or hard-of-hearing is that of acquiring the spoken language of the dominant culture, whether it be English or Spanish or Hindi. One must be facile with a spoken language in order to read and write using that language. Note that a person does not need to be able to speak a language to be literate in that language. The way most of us acquire language, however, is by being able to hear it as babies and then developing the spoken form. For children with a hearing impairment, developing the language of the dominant culture does not happen automatically as it does with people who hear. Given this, it follows that in our culture a student with a hearing impairment is likely to have difficulty with all phases of learning the English language.

Most students who are hearing impaired use a hearing aid. Some use a sign language interpreter. A major problem for hearing aid users is noise. Hearing aids amplify *all* sounds, not just speech. In a noisy classroom it is difficult to sort the speech from the background noise. Keep the classroom quiet. Usually a simple explanation to the class of how a hearing aid works will help students remember to keep quiet. Also, face the student when talking.

If a student uses a sign language interpreter, remember that an interpreter is just that—the interpreter is *not* the teacher or a tutor. An interpreter transmits spoken messages at a language level the hearing impaired child understands. It helps the interpreter to have copies of handouts, and to have prior notice if a film or tape is to be shown. The interpreter may want to review any media used. Be aware that if a classroom is darkened for a media presentation, there should be enough light for the interpreter to be seen. The eyes act as ears for a student who is hearing impaired.

Software Characteristics. Students with hearing impairments need software that will help them with language development. Software should include drill and practice with syntax and semantics. Hearing impaired students need practice in writing and reading for comprehension. Many students have gaps in their knowledge of English that may not be readily apparent. It is important to identify these gaps through the use of pretests and by collecting language samples and then proceeding accordingly.

Make certain that the directions for software use are written at a language level the student can understand. Check for generalization of skills. For example, the student may have been practicing on how to add "s" to make a plural. In the program the student gets all trials correct. Can the student then use plurals in written compositions correctly?

Learners Who Have a Communication Disorder

A student with a communication disorder may have problems with speech (fluency, voice quality, articulation) or language (expressive problems, receptive problems, language delay or absence of language). These students are uncomfortable communicating and/or cause discomfort in others. These students may be impaired because of cognitive dysfunction or because of physical problems such as a cleft palate or cerebral palsy. Communication disorders may range from mild to severe.

DEFINITION: Communication Disorder

Van Riper defines *speech disorders* as follows: "Speech is abnormal when it deviates so far from the speech of other people that it calls attention to itself, interferes with communication, or causes the speaker or his listener to be distressed" (1978, p. 43).

The American Speech-Language-Hearing Association (ASHA) defines *language impairment* as:

a state in which an individual does not display knowledge of the system of linguistic needs commensurate with the expected norm. Typically, a child is called language impaired when his/her skills in the primary language are deficient relative to expectations for chronological age.

Classroom Considerations/Accommodations. Students need to be put into situations that encourage unpressured communication with peers and adults. For students who have problems with language, opportunities to practice known skills are important so they can be used as a base for new skill development. Teachers should reinforce newly developing speech patterns.

Regular classroom teachers may be asked to reinforce aspects of therapy provided by the school's speech-language pathologist. A teacher's major responsibility is to provide a comfortable, nonthreatening atmosphere that encourages communication by the students. Teachers should also be accepting of assistive communication devices that may be needed in the classroom.

Software Characteristics. Students with severe speech problems may use assistive devices (these will be covered later in Chapter 7). Software should be used that reinforces goals set by the speech-language pathologist. Look for packages that specifically emphasize expressive language through typing or talking to the computer or receptive language through reading or listening to the computer.

Learners Who Have a Physical Impairment

The learner who is physically impaired has limited access to the environment because of a neurological disorder, a musculoskeletal disorder, or a health impairment (see Figure 1-9 for a list of these disorders). These disabilities may or may not be a handicapping condition. Students may be handicapped in one context but not in another. The cognitive and physical abilities range from above normal to severely impaired. Though children may fall into a specific disability category, their characteristics will vary widely. For example, two students with cerebral palsy may function quite differently. One student may be impaired in the ability to talk, but may function at a high cognitive level. Another student may have perfect facility for speaking but will function as a "slow learner." An important thing to remember is that a student may have profound physical limitations and still be very bright.

DEFINITION: Physical Impairment

The population of children with physical handicaps is very heterogeneous because it includes youngsters with many different conditions. Most of these conditions are unrelated, but for convenience they are often grouped into two categories: physical disabilities or health impairments. A physical disability results from a condition like cerebral palsy or a spinal cord injury that interferes with the child's ability to use his or her body. Many, but not all, physical disabilities are considered orthopedic impairments. (The term *orthopedic impairment* generally refers to conditions of the muscular or skeletal system, and sometimes to physically disabling conditions of the nervous system.) A condition like cystic fibrosis or diabetes that requires ongoing medical attention is a health impairment.

According to Section 504 of the Rehabilitation Act of 1973, a person is "handicapped" if he or she has a mental or physical impairment that substantially limits participation in one or more life activities. When a physical or health condition interferes with a child's ability to take part in routine school or home activities, the child has a physical handicap.

By this definition, a student who takes medication to control a health impairment is not physically handicapped. Nor is the student with an artificial arm who successfully takes part in all school activities, including physical education. But when a physical condition leaves a student unable to hold a pencil, to walk from class to class, to use conventional toilets—when it interferes with the student's participation in routine school activities— the child is physically handicapped. This does not mean the child cannot learn. But it does place a special responsibility on teachers and therapists to adapt materials and equipment to the student's needs, and to help the student learn to use these adaptations and to develop a strong self-concept.

Source: Rainforth (cited in Kirk & Gallagher, 1986, pp. 458–459).

Classroom Considerations/Accommodations. One of the most important things a teacher can do is to be accepting of a student with a physical impairment. The student may have no academic difficulties so the concern might be environmental accessibility, or allowing for the student's high level of fatigue, or making the environment safe. Figure 1-10 shows a special needs student using an alternative keyboard. The student and/or the special education consultant will have the

Figure 1-9
Physical disabilities.

NEUROLOGICAL	MUSCULOSKELETAL	CHRONIC ILLNESS AND OTHERS DISABILITIES
Cerebral palsy	Muscular dystrophy	Congenital malformations
Spina bifida	Arthrogryposis	Cystic fibrosis
Convulsive disorder	Legg-Perthes	Sickle cell anemia
Poliomyelitis	Osteogenesis imperfecta	Hemophilia
	Juvenile rheumatoid arthritis	Juvenile diabetes mellitus
	Scoliosis	Asthma
		Rheumatic fever

Source: Cartwright, Cartwright, & Ward, 1989, p. 182.

Figure 1-10
Student using an
alternative keyboard.
*Courtesy of Prentke
Romich Co.*

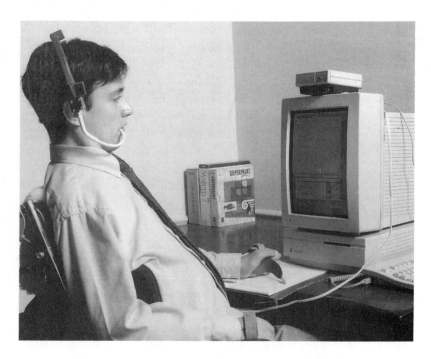

Figure 1-11
Teacher notes.

TEACHER NOTES

Kathy
 	
    Kathy has severe cerebral palsy, with major involvement of all four limbs. She is mainstreamed, but children don't interact with her. Her speech is poor. She sits at a computer workstation.
 	
    One way to make her an integral part of the class is to set up a situation in which Kathy's computer skill is needed by others in the class. For example, Kathy is now in charge of controlling the light in the reading corner with one of her switches, so the students need to ask her to turn the light on and off. She is also in charge of spelling and math computer games, which she is very familiar with. Students now crowd around her to play the games. To reduce the confusion students sign up to reserve specific times for computer games. Students are responsible for inserting the discs and returning them to the appropriate file. Kathy shows them how to work the software and plays the games with them.

information teachers and peers need about classroom considerations. Figure 1-11 shows teacher notes on Kathy, a child who has cerebral palsy.

The teacher's primary consideration for students with a physical impairment is to make the classroom physically accessible and to provide for peer group understanding and interaction. Accessibility may be as simple as arranging the classroom to accommodate a wheelchair or as complicated as setting up a center that consists of computer-controlled assistive devices.

Software Characteristics. Appropriate software choices will depend on what type of physical impairment is present. For those students who need help for physical movement only, see the section on assistive devices. For students with learning problems, identify the strengths and weaknesses (see other sections of software characteristics) and choose accordingly.

Learners Who Have Mental Retardation

The child who is classified as mentally retarded (MR) has deficits in cognitive function as well as deficits in adaptive behavior. In order for a child to be classified as MR a score value of 2 or more standard deviations below the mean (on an individually administered IQ test) must be made by the student *and* the student must have deficits in adaptive behavior. For example, a child who scores 2 or more SDs below the mean on an IQ test but who exhibits appropriate social and adaptive behavior as compared to his or her age-mates is *not* mentally retarded. The reverse is also true. A child who shows maladaptive behavior, but who scores within the normal range or above on an IQ test is also not retarded. This child would probably be classified as behavior disordered.

DEFINITION: Mental Retardation

Mental retardation refers to significantly subaverage general intellectual functioning existing concurrently with deficits in adaptive behavior and manifested during the developmental period. (Grossman, 1983, p. 1)

"Significantly subaverage general intellectual functioning" means that a child has a score on a standard intelligence test that is 2 or more standard deviations below the mean. "Deficits in adaptive behavior" is the failure to meet standards of independence and social responsibility expected of the individual's age and cultural group. The "developmental period" is the time from birth to age 18.

Classroom Considerations/Accommodations. Children with mental retardation reach the same developmental milestones as normal children; they just reach them at a later age. Children with mental retardation learn things more slowly, and both repetition and reinforcement are crucial. Students with retardation need more drill and practice than other students. They need an organized, structured learning environment, and multiple opportunities to generalize what they have learned. Social skills can be taught and reinforced through cooperative learning activities.

Students should have activities structured for success. Learning activities should be task analyzed in such a way that success is assured. Objectives should be broken down into small bites. Drill and practice should also be presented in small amounts. For example, the student should complete a math worksheet with five problems, not 25. Innovative evaluation techniques should be considered, such as drawing a picture rather than writing an essay or telling a story rather than writing answers to questions. The cognitive ability of students with retardation should be stretched. A good strategy is to use cooperative learning techniques as much as possible. Classmates can explain concepts and encourage and get creative responses from these students that teachers often miss.

Software Characteristics. Students with mental retardation will need software that uses a relatively uncluttered screen. Icons, pictures, and color will be helpful. Directions for software use should be at student's reading level. Check this carefully. Packages that allow drill and practice and promote cooperative learning are useful. If the student has poor fine motor skills, experiment with both a mouse and a keyboard to see which is easier to use.

Learners Who Have a Learning Disability

Students with learning disabilities are often called the puzzle children. As many as 99 characteristics have been listed for these children. Ultimately, children with learning disabilities are children who, in the presence of a normal IQ, are unable to learn through normal and traditional channels. A child with a learning disability may be performing at grade level in math but may be unable to read. A child with a learning disability may have problems with memory. He or she may acquire an academic skill one day and will have forgotten it the next. A child with a learning disability may be clumsy or have great difficulty paying attention to a task for more than a few seconds. A child with a learning disability may have difficulty with expressive language and/or receptive language; the child may be able to read but unable to write or read letters and numbers. Sequencing events could be a problem. A child with a learning disability may have a combination of many of the above characteristics. It is easy to imagine how a child with a learning disability would present a unique and baffling challenge to a teacher.

DEFINITION: Learning Disability

The term "children with specific learning disabilities" means those children who have a disorder in one or more of the basic psychological processes involved in understanding or in using language, spoken or written, which disorder may manifest itself in imperfect ability to listen, think, speak, read, write, spell, or to do mathematical calculations. Such disorders include such conditions as perceptual handicaps, brain injury, minimal brain dysfunction, dyslexia, and developmental aphasia. Such term does not include children who have learning problems which are primarily the result of visual, hearing, or motor handicaps, of mental retardation, of emotional disturbance, or of environmental, cultural, or economic disadvantage. (USOE, 1977, p. 65983)

Classroom Considerations/Accommodations. Given all the possible difficulties these children may have, it is difficult to summarize problems that will be encountered in the classroom. A teacher will need to choose one, some, or all of the following approaches. Some students will need clearcut behavioral and/or cognitive intervention. There are students who will need to have a learning task carefully analyzed and sequenced. And there are students who will need remediation, that is, they will need to relearn a skill correctly. Children who have attention disorders are often the most perplexing, because their inability to focus is out of their control. In fact, the worst thing that a person can say to a child with atten-

Figure 1-12
Teacher notes.

TEACHER NOTES

JOSH

Student Strengths:

1. Creative storyteller
2. Personable

What Needs Work:

1. Handwriting
2. Spelling
3. Getting thoughts onto paper
4. Can recognize simple words that he cannot spell

Try This:

1. Use word processing program with a word predictor component and a spelling checker.
2. Pair Josh with a friend at the computer. Tell them to compose an outrageous story about something they like, for example, baseball.
3. Demonstrate the software and turn them loose. Allow 15 minutes for the composition.
4. Working together, with Josh responsible for most of the typing, both students will become familiar with the program.
5. Have them print the story.
6. Check the story.
7. Back to the computer to make corrections.
8. Allow Josh to compose at the computer whenever possible.

---

tion problems is, "You could do that if you tried." Or, "If you would just pay attention you could do that." Children with attention problems truly cannot help it. There are strategies that can help these students. Some need medication. Others simply need a quiet place to work without auditory and visual distractions; a simple study carrel may help. Something all of these children need is experimenting with different learning strategies until one is found that may be successful. Children with learning disabilities benefit from well-planned, systematic teaching. Figure 1-12 shows teacher notes for Josh, a child who has a learning disability.

Organization for the student and the teacher is key. A student with a learning disability needs to know how his or her school day will unfold. This helps with transition from activity to activity. Build on student strengths. In cooperative learning activities have the student be responsible for things he or she is good at. Provide a distraction-free environment for tasks that are difficult for the student.

Software Characteristics. As a general rule children with a learning disability need things presented clearly and simply. Software should have an uncluttered screen presentation. Tasks should be well sequenced and broken down into small parts to allow one skill to be practiced and mastered before going to a higher-level skill. Do not assume that because a software program promises task analysis and skills practice that it will deliver that. It is always the teacher and the student who must decide if the software will provide what is needed. A simple but often overlooked strategy for software choice is to let the student make the evaluation. Teacher and students together can experiment with various packages. The students' feedback may give the teacher insight into how students are perceiving and responding to what they see. Doing this also gives students a feeling of power and responsibility for their own learning. Often experimentation is the only useful way to proceed because of the myriad learning problems these children may have.

Learners Who Have a Behavior Disorder

Students with behavior disorders exhibit chronic maladaptive behaviors. They may be overly aggressive or markedly withdrawn. Whatever the problem behavior, it must be exhibited to such a degree that it interferes with the student's academic progress and with his or her ability to develop and maintain satisfactory relationships with others.

DEFINITION: Behavior Disorder

PL 94-142, the Education for All Handicapped Children Act, defines behavior disabilities as a condition in which one or more of the following are exhibited to a marked degree or over a long period of time:

- An inability to learn which cannot be explained by intellectual, sensory or health factors.
- An inability to build or maintain satisfactory interpersonal relationships with peers or teachers.

Classroom Considerations/Accommodations. For whatever reason students with behavior disorders have usually experienced a lot of failure in the classroom. These students need success in academics and in interpersonal relationships. These students may show inconsistent behaviors. One day a math lesson may trigger an anxiety attack in a child. The next day the math lesson *and* the reading lesson cause problems. This creates stress for both teachers and students. These students often appear to be "slow learners" because their behavior has interfered with their schoolwork. It is difficult to do accurate evaluations of the student's cognitive functioning because the history of problem behaviors has confounded the student's ability to learn.

One approach in working with students with behavior disorders is structured, systematic, and consistent teaching. Usually these students have experienced cycles of failure that add to their frustration. Teachers must plan for success. Materials and assignments must be task analyzed in such a way that the student does not feel overwhelmed. The teacher and student must set up a behavior management plan and be consistent in implementing it. Consequences for appropriate and inappropriate behavior must be apparent and immediate.

Software Characteristics. Software for students with behavior disorders must be engaging. Students themselves are the best judges. For example, if a student needs practice in math, offer a choice of software. Allow the student to choose the one that looks the most interesting. The higher the level of interest in a task, the lower the probability the student will engage in inappropriate behaviors. Plan for success. The learning tasks must be at an appropriate level of difficulty. Check this carefully. Activities that use cooperative learning strategies at the computer are useful. There is enough structure to help students behave while they are having positive interactions with peers.

SUMMARY

Public Laws 94-142 and 101-476

PL 94-142 and 101-476, passed in 1975 and 1990 respectively, requires that students with disabilities be educated in the most appropriate, least restrictive environment (LRE). A team composed of parents, educators, the student, if appropriate, and/or specialists writes an IEP to be carried out by the education professionals. The promise was that students with disabilities had a legal right to be educated in the public schools. The hope was that education in the LRE would put students with disabilities into the mainstream of life rather than relegate them to the status of "outsiders." The reality is that many students with disabilities have benefited from the legislation and also that "LRE" is a complex concept that requires interpretation that is based as much on the spirit of the law as on its letter. Professionals must base decisions regarding LRE on individual student characteristics, not on disability categories.

Disability Characteristics

A student with a disability must be labeled according to a specific category (vision impaired, hearing impaired, communication disordered, physically disabled, mentally retarded, learning disabled, behavior disordered) in order to receive special education services. Definitions of each category have been provided, along with a general discussion of classroom considerations/accommodations and desirable software characteristics.

References

Algozzine, B., Maheady, L., Sacca, K., O'Shea, L., & O'Shea, D. (1990). Sometimes patent medicine works: A reply to Braaten, Kauffman, Braaten, Polsgrove, and Nelson. *Exceptional Children, 56,* 552–557.

Barraga, N. (1983). In S. A. Kirk & J. J. Gallagher (Eds.), *Educating exceptional children* (5th ed.). Boston: Houghton Mifflin.

Byrnes, M. (1990). The regular education initiative debate: A view from the field. *Exceptional Children, 56,* 345–349.

Cartwright, G. P., Cartwright, C. A., & Ward, M. E. (1989). *Educating special learners* (3rd ed.) (p. 182). Belmont, CA: Wadsworth Publishing Co.

Frisina, R. (1974). In S. A. Kirk & J. J. Gallagher (Eds.), *Educating exceptional children* (5th ed.). Boston: Houghton Mifflin.

Gajar, A. H. (1980). Characteristics across exceptional categories: EMR, LD, and ED. *Journal of Special Education, 14,* 165–173.

Grangreco, M. F., Dennis, R., Cloninger, C., Edelman, S., & Schattman, R. (1993). "I've counted Jon": Transformational experiences of teachers educating students with disabilities. *Exceptional Children, 59,* 359–371.

Grossman, H. (Ed.). (1983). In S. A. Kirk & J. J. Gallagher (Eds.), *Educating exceptional children* (5th ed.). Boston: Houghton Mifflin.

Hallahan, D. P., & Kauffman, J. M. (1977). Labels, categories, behaviors: ED, LD, and EMR reconsidered. *Journal of Special Education, 11,* 139–149.

Iran-Nejad, A., McKeachie, W. J., & Berliner, D. C. (1990). The multisource nature of learning: An introduction. *Review of Educational Research, 60,* 509–515.

Kauffman, J. (1977). *Characteristics of children's behavior disorders.* Columbus, OH: Charles E. Merrill.

Rainforth, B. (1986). In S. A. Kirk & J. J. Gallagher (Eds.), *Educating exceptional children* (5th ed.). Boston: Houghton Mifflin.

Truesdell, L. A., & Abramson, T. (1992). Academic behavior and grades of mainstreamed students with mild disabilities. *Exceptional Children, 58,* 392–397.

U.S. Office of Education (USOE). (1977). *Assistance to states for education of handicapped children: Procedures for evaluating specific learning disabilities* (*Federal Register, 42,* 65082–65082).

Van Riper, C. (1978). *Educating exceptional children* (5th ed.). Boston: Houghton Mifflin.

Wang, M., & Walberg, H. (1988). Four fallacies of segregationism. *Exceptional Children, 55,* 128–137.

York, J., Vandercook, T., MacDonald, C., Heise-Neff, C., & Caughey, E. (1992).

Feedback about integrating middle-school students with severe disabilities in general education classes. *Exceptional Children, 58,* 244–257.

Zigmond, N., & Baker, J. (1990). Mainstream experience for learning disabled students (Project MELD): Preliminary report. *Exceptional Children, 57,* 176–185.

People Who Help Support/Multidisciplinary Teams

Objectives

After reading this chapter, you should be able to:

- Identify key elements of the referral process for the learner with special needs.
- Describe the primary responsibilities of members of the support/multidisciplinary team.
- Describe specific roles for the teachers and administrators on the team.
- Identify the major purposes of a staff development program.
- Identify the key reason for having a strong site-based administrative program relative to instruction for the learner with special needs.
- Describe the use of self-assessment tools in working with students with special needs.

The student with special needs may require assistance in the pursuit of his or her educational opportunities. Special groups of people are responsible for programmatic decisions relative to the academic progress of this student. As has been determined, the student with special needs must be identified as having some problem that could potentially cause a need for special services.

Students who are eligible for special education services are identified by professional staff members and/or other persons with knowledge or expertise in the needs area. Before services can be delivered, this identification process must occur. The formal referral may be made by parents, school personnel, or any concerned persons. It may come about because of prior information about or performance by the child.

Initiative for referral may be taken by parents (guardian, etc.). If the parents are denied referral by the school, they are entitled to a formal hearing. If the school initiates the referral, parents must be informed and written consent obtained before initiating the process. If the parents refuse to give consent, the school may request a hearing.

Within a specific number of days after the referral, a person must be chosen as the multidisciplinary team (M-team) chairperson. This person is responsible for obtaining written, informed parental consent and identifying the remaining members of the M-team. Individual assessment personnel, parents, and (when appropriate), the student should serve on the M-team. One member of the M-team should be knowledgeable about the suspected disability being assessed. Parents must give their consent before an initial assessment can be conducted. After the M-team is formed and parental consent is obtained, a comprehensive evaluation may begin. Its purpose is to collect data that will enable the M-team to make decisions about the student's needs for special education and/or related services. Members make written, individual assessments and present them in an M-team meeting. These assessments should provide both descriptive and prescriptive information, with the provision that no single instrument, item of equipment, or the like can be used to determine a child's eligibility.

The descriptive information reports behaviors as observed in the classroom (unless the child is homebound, speech impaired, or not previously enrolled in school) as well as the child's limitations, deficits, and strengths.

Prescriptive information includes recommendations, goals, and objectives from which IEPs can be written. Components of a tentative IEP are developed from this integrated assessment. (See Figure 2-1 for a sample IEP written with a software package designed for this purpose. See Appendix B for a description of the PennStar IEP Manager.)

Another important issue in this comprehensive evaluation is nondiscriminatory testing procedures and instruments. The tests must have proven validity, must be in the child's native language, and must be administered by a person who

Figure 2-1
Individual Education
Program (IEP).

NAME: Megan Smith   DOB: 06/03/82

SPECIAL EDUCATION ASSIGNMENT LEVEL AND LOCATION OF INTERVENTION	START DATE	EXPECTED DURATION	TIME/ WEEK
Elementary Learning Support	9/25/91	9/25/92	5x

EXPLANATION OF REGULAR EDUCATION INTEGRATION
Attend regular education classes except reading, language arts, and spelling.

RELATED SERVICES	MINS. PER SESSION	START DATE	EXPECTED DURATION	FREQ.
Transportation (Regular)	30	9/25/91	9/25/92	10x

PHYSICAL EDUCATION: Regular

SPECIAL MEDIA AND MATERIALS
Tests will be read aloud.

SPECIALLY-DESIGNED INSTRUCTION
A. Use increased repetitions across variety of persons and places to increase rate of retention and promote generalization. B. Use auditory cues for content areas (read content area materials to student). C. Ask student to read into a tape recorder and listen to playback of what she has read for meaning and content. D. Read tests aloud to student. E. Use computer programs which integrate reading, spelling, and language arts. F. Use curriculum-based assessment (CBA) as an instructional technique. G. Use instructional techniques to highlight and reinforce differences between letters 'b' and 'd'.

NOTE: A version of this sample IEP appears on page 56 of the MDE/IEP GUIDELINES.

EXTENDED SCHOOL YEAR ELIGIBILITY: No

IEP PLANNING PARTICIPANTS   MEETING DATE: 09/20/91

TEACHER: Joan Slade, 3rd Grade

PARENT: Linda Smith

LEA/REP: Thomas Jones, Principal

Teacher: Ann Williams, Lrng. Spt.

PRESENT EDUCATIONAL LEVELS
Reading--middle of first grade reader
Math--within grade level
Sight vocabulary and work attack skills are below grade level
Difficulties in spelling and language arts
Comprehends when words are read to her
Able to develop ideas independently
Rate of retention is significantly below grade level

Additional annual goal:
Communicate orally and in writing in order to meet the demands of the regular education curriculum.

ANNUAL GOAL: Read and comprehend at grade level

EXIT CRITERIA
Megan will no longer be eligible for special education when she is able to accomplish the goals and objectives listed in the IEP without support.

****
Planned Courses in all curricular areas are available upon request.
****

SHORT TERM OBJECTIVES

Reads 2nd grade materials; with fluency of 60 WPM; with 93-97% accuracy; as indicated by daily curriculum-based assessment

Comprehends what is read; with 80% accuracy; as indicated by daily curriculum-based assessment

Spells known words from reading curriculum; with 93-97% accuracy; as indicated by daily curriculum-based assessment

Uses word attack skills, capitalization, punctuation; from 2nd grade curriculum, in basic sentences, paragraphs; with 93-97% accuracy; as indicated by daily curriculum-based assessment

Increases rate of retention; through increased repetition; to the 95% level; as indicated by daily curriculum-based assessment

Does not reverse letters 'b' and 'd'; with 93-97% accuracy; as indicated by daily curriculum-based assessment

This IEP was created on the PennStar IEP Manager Version 2.5.

is trained in using them. No one test may be used as the sole determining factor in deciding how and where a child should be placed. The testing must not be limited to IQ tests; also, tests must reflect aptitude and achievement, not just impairments. Evaluations must be made by a group such as the M-team that has at least one member who is knowledgeable about the suspected disability. All areas related to the suspected disability should be tested, including health, vision, hearing, emotional status, communication abilities, and academic performance. After the individual assessments are made, the M-team provides an integrated assessment report. The written report of each individual assessment should include the following elements.

First, there should be a statement concerning any physical or mental impairments revealed by the testing that form a basis for determining eligibility. Second, any relevant observable behaviors that relate to academic performance and functioning should be reported. Third, any educationally relevant medical findings should be included. Fourth, any severe discrepancy between a child's age, grade level, and ability and his or her performance or achievement should be explained. Finally, environmental, cultural, and social factors that may influence assessment outcomes should be addressed.

This integrated report is signed by all members of the M-team, regardless of whether or not they agree. If members disagree, they are allowed to file a minority report stating areas and reasons for disagreement. If parents disagree with the findings, a due process hearing may be requested. A summary of this report is given to parents whether the child is found eligible for special education and related services or not. Test materials and any other assessment information must be filed.

The M-team then develops and writes an IEP and makes placement recommendations. Within 30 days after the child is deemed eligible for special education or related services, the M-team meets to review and revise the original IEP. The M-team must meet at least once each year to review/revise the IEP, allowing for requests by the parents. Parents must be provided a written notice of eligibility for their child if the parents are not present. Also, written consent forms may be mailed to parents to obtain permission for initial placement. An IEP or the status of the child cannot be changed for 14 days without written, informed parental consent. It is always good practice to get parents involved in every phase of this process. The more invested the family is in providing services, the higher the probability that the student will benefit from services.

Teachers

In general, this text takes the position that teachers are users, not producers, of computer programs. The classroom teacher, while certainly capable of producing high-quality and important programming efforts, rarely has the time to produce such work. Rather, the teacher should be concerned about having available the best quality software to use with the appropriate adaptive device and sufficient computer power to accomplish the necessary teaching/learning goals.

The critical role the teacher has in dealing with students with special needs is a magnification of the role that the teacher has in dealing with all students. For example, a learner without a disability may need teacher-generated materials, a separate place to work, and instructions. This book deals with the student who needs these things, but also needs additional assistance from a teacher or some other individual, such as another student, an aide, a parent, or a system resource person. This additional assistance is needed to enhance utilization of an assistive device or a series of assistive devices that enable that particular youngster to reach the point where learning can begin to take place.

Ideally, lessons need to be constructed that are sensitive to the learning style of each individual child, meet the educational objectives of that particular set, and also meet the educational objectives of the learner. The learner may have a difficult time assimilating, questioning, or providing feedback or dealing with any of the things that are normally associated with "regular" learning. The need to learn students with special needs have is no different from the need to learn students without disabilities have. However, the presence of assistive devices for students with mental, physical, behavioral, or communication disabilities will provide more of a challenge and in many instances substantially more frustrations for the teacher and other students. Additional complications may arise if assistive devices are required for one group of learners but not another group. There is no learner who does not need some assistance. The issue of whether the teacher can provide substantial assistance is always a question.

Developing an instructional plan requires considering the students and their learning styles, the capability of each instructional medium or tool, and the purpose, role, and limitations of assistive devices. The computer can be a powerful instructional tool for the teacher—assuming the instructional plan can be properly utilized, the material can be properly adapted for use on a computer, the use of the assistive device can be taught, and the assistive device can be programmed into the regular instructional program. A basic question is, How can the computer and the appropriate assistive devices help an instructor be a better teacher than he or she would be without that device or computer?

The computer should be viewed as simply another instructional support item for the student and teacher to use as the student attempts to learn and as the teacher attempts to teach. It is important for the teacher to note that the presence or absence of assistive devices as well as the presence or absence of a computer and, as a matter of fact, the presence or absence of workbooks, videotapes, or tape recorders are not necessarily a detriment to the instructional program of a school. The computer is one of a series of tools, if not the most dominant tool, available to teachers in providing multiple formats, different levels of instruction, the integration of assistive devices to provide certain levels of instruction, classroom performance monitoring process, and record keeping.

When instruction is considered, the teacher must allow for a wide diversity of learner needs and approaches while maintaining both a basic direction of instructional intent and a basic credibility of instructional content. The diversity brought to a classroom with special needs learners is but one of many factors that affect teaching and learning.

Staff Development

The final responsibility for any instruction rests with the individual teacher. Regardless of the support provided for individual instructors, the quantity of assistive devices, the quality of the software, or the ability of the learner, the final "line of defense" rests with the teacher. A school district's or system's ability to provide support may be a key, but the training and drive to use such support are up to each instructor.

Staff development is a major concern for all aspects of education, and computer work is no exception. Overcoming initial resistance to computers or any other new idea or system is a problem for all site-based administrators or system-based personnel. Most teachers receiving licensure in the next five to 10 years can be expected to have at least a minimum degree of computer literacy and some exposure to packaged software. Few will have had programming experience, although a limited number may have had a demonstration of LOGO activities for use in classrooms. The degree of computer literacy of more experienced teachers is an unknown. However, to assume that more experienced teachers are always resistant to working with the computer is not correct. Many of them have enthusiastically embraced the computer and its multiple uses. Generally, these uses fall into three areas: direct intervention; management of instructional and other student data; and student assessment and diagnosis. Most software applications will fit one of these three areas.

One of the many things the teacher must guard against is overdependence on the computer and an assistive device or devices rather than remembering that good teaching practices for any student are probably good teaching practices for students with special needs with the proper modifications of set, structure, or evaluative criteria. The tendency to "fall in love" with the computer or the assistive device is easy. The ability to put these items of hardware and the accompanying software products in proper prospective is a challenge for the teacher, resource person, and administrator.

Administrators

While it is true that there is at least one level of personnel between an individual child with special needs and the school administrator, the administrator has a major role in the success of each teacher and each pupil. Clearly, the principal or other school site administrator represents a major level of needs interpretation and empowerment as well as a major interface between the child and the parent.

Most school situations reflect a traditional top-down administrative style—with lots of information flowing down and little information flowing back. Many systems operate with a substantial staff of supervisors and administrators based at a central site with oversight responsibilities and little day-to-day contact with pupils or parents. In many instances this arrangement works well, and appropriate services are provided for pupils and faculty.

Site-Based Management

One of the more popular ideas in education today involves a form of site-based management. In this approach, at least some of the decisions about budget, curriculum, staffing, and organization of programs are left up to the local building administrator and the staff rather than the central office. Basically, in the central office model of management, all decisions are centralized and applied to all sites. In the site-based approach, at least some of the important decisions are made at the site and reflect the unique characteristics of the site, the faculty, the community, and the student body. Both ideas have merit; the decision about which model is appropriate is based on a number of factors.

The idea of determining programs and procedures with local input is interesting and intriguing. However, site-based management makes for a lot of decisions and a lot of differences. Some of these differences may be at best substantial and at worst controversial. Superintendents and other central office staff must be willing to live with the loss of control (perceived or actual) and with the loss of budget control. This latter problem is most often difficult for central office administrators and in some instances for principals with little or no experience in budget control and its attendant problems.

The administration of a school is at best a complex task. The administration of a school serving multiple populations (ethnic, special services, etc.) makes the task even more complicated. With the current, continuing concern fostered by budget woes, family situations, and the pressure for academic success, school administrators face important issues with the day-to-day functions of managing the building, as well as the pressures for long-term success. Instructional leadership and management often clash over the demands on time and how to make the best use of it.

There is little if any question that site-based management is the wave of the future for administration of local schools. While growth of the idea has been slowed by the unsettled economic conditions of recent years, the push to give more and more autonomy to local-site principals is irreversible. Persons on the day-to-day "firing line" at a school site often have a substantially better feel for their "clients" and their clients' needs than do administrators in a central office. Without question, certain decisions need to be centralized and a common approval procedure used by all sites. Other decisions are more appropriately made at the local level. Boards of education must provide policy guidelines to provide a framework for determining parameters for decision making. The site-based administrator must have the authority to make decisions within board policy guidelines and expect that these decisions will be supported. Decisions will have both successful and unsuccessful outcomes. Site-based management is designed to make decisions occur sooner and to be most responsive to local input. The needs of individual learners, special needs or not, arguably are better met with direct input from the first-line workers—local teachers, aides, parents, students, and administrators—rather than delaying decisions until information can be transferred to another site, processed, and returned.

One of the key functions of site-based administration is to integrate all human resources into the program at a local school. The real purpose of choosing the word *site* is to reflect the idea that a site is substantially more than just a building. It consists of the land, buildings, equipment, and—more important—the human resources (both paid and volunteer, locally assigned or tangentially related staff/faculty from the central office). The concept of the community as "site" is a major plus in any setting, but especially as a support service for students with special needs. The flexibility available to the site administrator is a crucial factor—especially during times of scarce resources—in extending the educational learning and experience base of all learners. (An excellent reference work on site-based management is Candoli's *School District Administration: Strategic Planning for Site-Based Management.*)

Special Faculty/Staff

PL 100-407, Technology-Related Assistance for Individuals with Disabilities Act of 1988, calls for "trained personnel to provide such decisions and services and to assist individuals with disabilities to use such devices and services."

This impetus should provide enough incentive to a school district to provide not only appropriate devices but also the trained personnel needed to work with students, staff, and faculty in the implementation of such devices. The average or even the most advanced school system will not have enough trained personnel to facilitate these activities to the degree necessary for full implementation of the intent of the law. Many—if not all—states lack comprehensive programs for making available technology-selection assistance to individuals with disabilities. Additionally, there is a lack of coordination among existing federal, state, and private agencies for the information and support that do exist.

Regardless of these problems, the need exists for schools to serve students with disabilities. Thus, if expertise is not available, school systems have the responsibility of finding appropriately trained persons or training such personnel. Corporate groups like IBM, Apple, and many others are willing and eager to illustrate the use of assistive devices with hardware they sell. One of the difficulties of securing training on assistive devices is the fact that many of these devices are produced by small companies with only a few products. Therefore, their budget for training and/or their staff available for training is substantially limited.

Schools must decide who needs to be trained and how that training should be meshed with other staff development work in the district. The size of the district and the breadth of programs will dictate the scope and direction of training. Plans for training or staff development must always allow for distribution of what is learned to other appropriate members of the faculty or staff across the district.

Additionally, the choice of what training should be sought and in what order are important considerations. It may well be a "juggling act" on the part of a district or school to provide the most appropriate training. However, eventually all appropriate training must be obtained/provided and all types of disabilities must be served. The training program, whether for classroom teachers or for system-wide resource persons, must be an integral part of the service delivery system.

Self-Assessment Tools

There is a continuing need for teachers (and other professionals) to assess themselves relative to their level of knowledge in many areas. Technology is certainly one of these. The "Technical Competencies for Special Education Teachers, Self-Assessment" by A. Edward Blackhurst of the University of Kentucky's Department of Special Education provides checklists, scales, and other instruments that are useful for independent, self-help work. (This instrument appears in Appendix C.)

In August 1988 Congress passed PL 100-407, the Technology-Related Assistance for Individuals with Disabilities Act. A primary purpose of the act was to provide financial assistance to enable each state to develop and implement a consumer-responsive, comprehensive state-wide program of technology-related assistance for individuals of all ages with disabilities. The act was designed to systematically expand the availability of assistive technology services and devices to these individuals through the provision of a discretionary state grant program.

The act offered a vitally important opportunity to address the deficiencies and gaps especially related to assistive technology services. The legislative mandate was to plan and implement consumer-responsive state-wide delivery systems based on meaningful interagency coordination and supported by creative funding initiatives.

Summary

This chapter has dealt with the work of support/multidisciplinary teams and their relationship to instructional delivery. The second major section of the chapter examines the many aspects of the role of the teacher in the instructional process, including selection, development, and support. The role of administrators in the instructional process and the increasing importance of site-based management are noted. The chapter concludes with a discussion of the role of special faculty/staff and the use of self-assessment tools.

References

Candoli, I. C. (1990). *School district administration: Strategic planning for site based management.* Lancaster, PA: Technomics Publishing.

PL 100-407. (1988, August). 100th Congress.

Learning and Instruction

Objectives

After reading this chapter, you should be able to:

*   Describe issues relevant to computer integration into classrooms.
*   Describe four types of classroom applications for computers.
*   Describe three instructional delivery formats: cooperative, competitive, and individualistic.
*   Describe issues in service delivery.
*   Describe testing accommodations for persons with disabilities.

A critical issue in educational settings continues to be the degree of effectiveness of the instruction provided for students with special needs. Clearly the concern for instructional effectiveness is not limited to these students, but covers all learners. The use of computers is but one of many instructional schemes available to a creative teacher for use with all students. Assistive hardware devices and adaptable software have opened the door to independent learning and living for many students with mental, physical, behavioral, and other disabilities. However, the involvement of a competent teacher is a must for the successful, effective, and efficient use of both hardware and software.

Key factors to consider in any instructional plan—for nondisabled students or for students with disabilities—are the determination of instructional goals, the implementation plan, and expected student outcomes. Assessment of student progress is critical for determination of what the student is not learning and what student strengths are.

Computers and Learning

One description of the way humans learn parallels the general information-processing model: (1) receiving information; (2) retaining, retrieving, and processing information; and (3) responding to information (Simon & Feigenbaum, 1964). This model is similar to the way a computer functions. The computer allows—especially with the possibility of such variable input formats as numbers, text, or pictures—for valuable support of instruction for students with special needs. (See Appendix D for an explanation of Computer Basics.) The many assistive devices, including switches, pointers, speech synthesizers, braille printers, key guards, touch-sensitive sleeves, alternative keyboards, voice recognition systems, and light pens, allow the computer to reserve and retain information for present or later processing and outputting.

The keys to computer integration in the classroom are teacher acceptance of the machine(s) and assistive hardware devices and the careful selection of appropriate software. Teacher acceptance allows for the basic adaptation of the hardware to support the student or at least allows the student to utilize the computer in his or her own environment. Careful selection of software allows for the appropriate level and type of instruction to be presented. The ability to secure assistive devices for use in the classroom, computer lab, or home has made the concept of a mainstreamed program take on day-to-day reality for the teacher, the school, the school system, and, most especially, the individual learner.

Identification and acquisition of the appropriate assistive device are crucial. In addition, instruction and training for teachers, administrators, resource persons, and parents in the appropriate and inappropriate use of assistive devices must be part of any educational plan. Accessibility for students and teachers is

Figure 3-1
Student computer
interaction. *Courtesy of
Apple Computer, Inc.*

another key to the proper integration of assistive devices into the instructional
program of individual students.

Anyone can purchase and use most software packages, but training is
necessary to select and effectively integrate appropriate software packages into

Figure 3-2
The Apple IIGS with
AppleColor RGB
Monitor, Apple 3.5
Drive, and ImageWriter
Printer. *Courtesy of
Apple Computer, Inc.*

Figure 3-3
Systems approach model
for designing instruction.
Source: Systematic
Design of Instruction,
Walter Dick & Lou Carey.

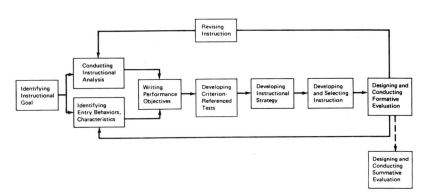

Figure 3-3
Systems approach model
for designing instruction.
Source: Systematic
Design of Instruction,
Walter Dick & Lou Carey.

an educational experience for students. With the tremendous growth of the software industry and the cost of software packages, the ability to select effective, efficient packages for students with special needs is especially challenging. Choosing and utilizing software and the appropriate adaptive devices to provide an appropriate learning experience is a difficult task (Watkins, 1991).

The effectiveness of the computer as an instructional tool is directly proportional to the quality of the instructional content. Computers do not make weak instructional content strong. When designing a computer instructional module, lesson, or course, all important components in any instructional design must be considered. While there is no instructional design model that seems to be "the best," the Instructional Design Model from Walter Dick and Lou Carey as illustrated in Figure 3-3 presents a excellent guide (Dick & Carey, 1978).

Classroom Applications for Computers

Most often computers are used in a direct, one-to-one approach, that is, one person working at one machine. More opportunities than this one-dimensional approach are explained below. For example, Figure 3-4 shows four levels of computer use:

1. Enhancing existing materials and approaches
2. Using existing software
3. Adapting existing software and videodiscs
4. Creating original courseware

While originally conceived as support of college and university work, these ideas translate easily into work with pupils with special needs.

During the past decade, computers have come to play a major role in teaching and learning in higher education. The concept of integrating technology into

Figure 3-4
Four levels of
computer use.

FOUR LEVELS OF COMPUTER USE

COMPUTER USE	TEACHING MODES		
	Lecture/ Presentation	Collaboration	Classroom-independent Instruction
• **Enhancing existing materials and approaches:** Using tools such as word processors and presentation software to create more professional lecture notes, class handouts, and classroom presentations.	Word processing, presentation and outlining software, electronically distributed or projected	Facilitates editing of team-taught materials	Word-processed class hand-outs, notes
• **Using existing software:** Taking advantage of commercially available software, from basic productivity tools to discipline-specific packages, to help with both your teaching and your students' learning.	Using courseware or productivity tools for lecture/ presentation	Using collaboration, networked writing and communications software	Using courseware, self-paced tutorials, drill and test packages
• **Adapting existing software and videodiscs:** Altering or adding to available computer-based materials to introduce content specific to a particular course or teaching approach.	Diversifying the use of video and multimedia packages, using HyperCard or other authoring tools	Altering or adapting on-line simulations through group participation	Diversifying the use of video and other media for drills, tutorials, and simulations
• **Creating original courseware:** Developing your own computer-based instructional materials, using authoring tools such as HyperCard or a programming language.	Developing custom lecture packages using programming or authoring tools	Modification and creation of new software by a group over a network	Developing custom self-paced materials

instruction means various things to various persons. The integration activities range from simple to complex and from a single activity to a total instructional program.

Some people feel that any use of computers qualifies as technology integration, while others define "integration" much more strictly. The latter group believes that technology is not truly integrated into instruction unless it has a powerful impact on teaching and learning experiences within classes.

There are many approaches to instructional use of computers, ranging from enhancing traditional teaching techniques to supporting entirely new modes of learning. Listed below are four of the most prominent ones.

Enhancing Existing Materials and Approaches

At the most basic level, a computer can help instructors do what they've always done—only better. Word-processing software makes it easy to revise course materials and lecture notes to incorporate new information or insights, as well as to make such materials more attractive and accessible. Computers can also be used to generate professional-quality lecture materials, such as overhead transparencies and 35 mm slides. Such tools serve two major instructional functions: to emphasize points and to add graphic material.

In addition, a computer connected to a projector can serve as a "dynamic" blackboard, allowing for change as needed to support instructional activity. Not only can it be used to illustrate the points covered in a lecture; it also allows for spur-of-the moment adjustments and immediate response to student questions or other input.

Using Existing Software

One of the early barriers to more widespread use of computers in education was the misconception that, in order to make effective use of computers, it was necessary to know how to program them. (Because of the initial scarcity of instructionally oriented software, there was more than a little truth to this.) Today, however, the notion that programming skills are a necessary prerequisite to instructional computer use is clearly untrue. A wide variety of software is commercially available that is applicable to an even wider variety of academic disciplines.

In addition to generally available productivity tools such as word-processing packages, spreadsheets, and the like, many instructors who would still never think of "programming" a computer make use of software that was originally created by their peers and is now available commercially. A more recent trend that has made another crop of courseware more widely accessible is the bundling of software with textbooks. Through drill and practice, tutorials, or exploratory exercises, instructors who adopt these textbooks can easily integrate use

Figure 3-5
Teacher notes.

> **TEACHER NOTES**
>
> **"A Way to Introduce Computer Use to a Class."**
>
> Steps: 1. Connect computer to large-screen TV.
>   2. Use Crossword Magic Program.
>   3. Explain that students can create crossword puzzles.
>   4. Ask students to supply words and definitions.
>   5. Example: student gives word "red."
>   *Definition*:   students brainstorm
>   fire engine—but can be green
>   apple—but can be green also
>   Finally students decide that STOP signs are always red.
>   So definition = the color of a stop sign.
>
>   Example: student gives word "dog."
>   *Definition*:   students brainstorm
>   an animal—but many animals
>   it barks—but seals bark also
>   domesticated animal—an animal that lives in
>   a home, but cats are also domesticated
>   Finally, definition = a domesticated animal that barks.
>   6. Meantime: someone keys in words and definitions.
>   7. Program produces puzzle, everyone gets hard copy.
>   8. Can reference hard copy for specific words and how to
>   spell them and complete the puzzle.
>
> **GOAL**
>
> Activity provides:
>
> 1. experience in brainstorming (convergent thinking).
> 2. reference for spelling of known words—can be used later in composi-
>   tions.

of the bundled software into their classroom instruction or their students' lab activities.

Adapting Existing Software and Videodiscs

The third stage of technology use consists of adapting existing materials to work within a specific curriculum. This can be as simple as creating spreadsheet-based templates that deal with discipline-specific problems, or as complex as developing software that provides a discipline-specific context using an existing videodisc.

The proliferation of discipline-specific HyperText stacks has led to another broad area of adaptation of existing materials. A number of relatively nontechni-

37 SUBSCRIPTIONS				$100.00 ORIGINAL BUDGET			
07/01/93–06/30/94		1993–1994		$100.00 REVISED BUDGET			
						BUDGET	
DATE	DESCRIPTION	EXPENDITURES	TOTAL	CREDITS	TOTAL	REVISION	BALANCE
JULY							
AUGUST							$100.00
SEPTEMBER							$100.00
10/09 Education Week 1/13/94–							
1/13/95		$59.94					$40.06
		MO.TOTAL	$59.94	$0.00			$40.06
		TO/DATE/TOTAL	$59.94	$0.00			$40.06
OCTOBER							$40.06
NOVEMBER							$40.06

Figure 3-6
Spreadsheet.

cal instructors, who would still never dream of "developing courseware," happily alter HyperText stacks developed by others to suit their specific instructional needs.

DEFINITION: HyperCard

HyperCard (an Apple Computer specific program) allows a teacher to create computer-based materials without learning to program. Such materials are called "stacks"; each stack is a collection of cards (a card can be seen as one screen of material). A detailed explanation of HyperCard appears later in this text.

The adaptation of existing videodiscs is a slightly more involved process— but, again, thanks to programs such as HyperCard, only slightly. Commercial videodiscs are available on a wide variety of topics, from the worlds of art in the National Gallery to basic biological processes. Many instructors have used HyperCard to create stacks that provide instructional context for specific video images.

Creating Original Courseware

At one time developing a software package required years of practice writing programs. Today, because of the ease of use of HyperCard and other authoring programs, it's a short step from adapting existing materials to creating your own. In the five years since HyperCard made its debut, scores of instructors have tapped their subject-matter expertise to create their own instructional software—everything from the simplest of drill-and-practice exercises to the most complex of interactive multimedia simulations.

Learner Goals

The need to establish individual, time-oriented goals and short-term objectives for all learners, especially for learners with special needs, is generally accepted and was noted in previous paragraphs. Writing an IEP is a difficult and time-consuming task. Distinguishing between difficult to measure learning goals and subject-specific objectives presents major challenges to teachers.

Instructional Delivery Formats

Once IEPs are written and regular class goals and objectives established, teachers can use computers in the classroom to augment cooperative, individualistic, and competitive instructional formats to meet educational goals.

Following are definitions of these formats and suggestions on how to implement them using computers. Much of the information on these three types of learning is developed from the work of Johnson and Johnson (1991).

Cooperative Learning

Cooperative learning can be described as two or more students working together to achieve a shared goal. Each person maximizes his or her achievement and each person succeeds only when the group succeeds.

There is a useful body of research on cooperative learning as it relates to computer use in schools, and with mainstreamed students. Watson (1991–1992), after setting up a computer lab in an elementary school, decided to place students in pairs at the computer. He did this because:

1. Students working in pairs seemed to do better work.
2. Students working in pairs appeared to be more capable of solving their own problems and less in need of teacher assistance.
3. Students working in pairs seemed to be on-task more of the time and to have greater on-task endurance. (p. 5)

Other research suggests that group computer use seems to enhance friendships, promote on-task behavior, and in some cases improve academic achievement (Watson, 1991–1992), enriching the life of mainstreamed students in the regular classroom.

Cooperative learning strategies employing computers should enhance the interaction of students who have disabilities with those who do not. For these kinds of learning activities to succeed, however, teachers need to assign roles to each student relative to different tasks, outline clear academic and/or social goals, and make clear to the students that interdependence is the way to achieve what they want to accomplish. Using jigsaw (Kagan, 1989) as a structure is one example. (Jigsaw requires students to become experts on one part of the task, and then teach that part to the other group members.) The mainstreamed student is allowed to get help to learn his or her part of the task. Another example may be each member being assigned different goals for a task. For example, student A may be expected to get all problems correct. Student B is to get five more correct than the day before.

One review of the research on the effects of cooperative learning and the academic achievement of students with disabilities (Tateyama-Sniezek, 1990) found there was no clear-cut evidence that cooperative learning helped mainstreamed students. The research reviewed, however, did not include cooperative learning at the computer. Teachers themselves can make judgments on academic improvement and increased socialization for mainstreamed students until definitive research comes out. It is clear that task structure and incentive structures must be experimented with in various group arrangements until the optimum learning of all students is achieved.

There is a strong caveat for teachers that goes against accepted conventional wisdom: children do *not* need drill and mastery of basics before they are capable of problem solving or higher-order thinking (Sutton, 1991). It is wrong to assume a mainstreamed student cannot achieve complex learning. "Prerequisite skills" are not necessary unless they are true prerequisites to understanding a concept (e.g., one need not know how to subtract in order to multiply, though subtraction is always taught prior to multiplication).

Individualistic Learning

In individualistic learning the student works independently, interacting only with the teacher who serves as a resource person. The task must be clearly defined. The student works to a specific criterion level (i.e., the student's work is not compared to another student's work). All materials necessary are in the student's possession. The student has a workplace relatively free of distraction. The student knows what is learned will be required in a future cooperative learning situation. Simple skills or knowledge acquisition tasks are most appropriate for individualistic efforts.

A computer station provides an ideal environment for individualistic learning activities, provided the software allows the student to work on the desired skills. Remember, individualistic learning requires that students work strictly on their own using only teacher assistance and that students be able to ignore distractions.

Many software programs are designed to present simple skills and basic knowledge, and many allow the student to work more independently with less teacher assistance. These programs also have drill and practice activities. Teachers and/or students can also use the computer to record answers to make record keeping (e.g., whether or not the student reached criterion level performance) easier.

An important thing to remember is that students must believe their individualistic learning tasks are relevant and that they will be called on at a later date to use what they have learned.

Competitive Learning

Competitive learning situations are appropriate only when they lead to constructive outcomes. Competitive situations should be set up to practice *known* skills or to review basic knowledge only. These situations are constructive when everyone has an equal chance of winning and when the atmosphere is such that students don't mind losing. "Whenever possible, make competition intergroup rather than interpersonal" (Johnson & Johnson, 1991, p. 104). Students with disabilities should have a higher probability of succeeding in competition if they are members of a team that has nondisabled members. Being part of a team also enhances development of social skills and allows team members to view themselves a part of a competent whole. The disability may fade into insignificance; what counts is what you know.

An example of a competition that involves computer use follows. Each team is at a computer. The game is based on accessing information from a specific software program. The object of the game is to find the answer in the shortest amount of time. The teacher presents 10 questions. The team that accesses and answers the 10 questions in the least amount of time wins. This game not only reviews specific knowledge but also allows practice in using the computer.

Service Delivery

One of the key features of working in a classroom with pupils having various disabilities is the perceived—rather than real—need to be "all things to all people." While differences do exist when working in a mainstreamed classroom, one purpose of this text is to show how the same adaptive device, when utilized

PLACEMENT	Mental Retardation	Learning Disability	Physical Impairment	Hearing Impairment	Communication Disorder	Behavior Disorder	Visual Impairment
RESIDENTIAL (Level 1)	B,C		B,C	C		C	C
DAY SCHOOL (Level 2)	B,C	C	B,C	C		C	C
SPECIAL CLASS (Level 3)	B,C	B,C	B,C	C	C	C	C
PART-TIME IN REGULAR CLASS (Level 4)	A,B	B,C	B,C	B,C	C	B,C	B,C
SUPPORT SERVICES FOR REGULAR EDUCATION TEACHER (Level 5)	A,B	A,B	A,B,C	A,B,C	B,C,	B	B,C
CONSULTING FOR REGULAR EDUCATION TEACHERS (Level 6)	A	A,B	A,B,C	A,B,C	B,C	A,B	A,B,C
REGULAR CLASS (Level 7)	A	A,B	A,B,C	A,B,C	A,B,C	A,B	A,B,C

A = MILD; B = MODERATE; C = SEVERE

Figure 3-7
Special services, likely level, and support federal categories of disability. *Source:* Adapted from Cascade of Services - G.P. Cartwright, C.A. Cartwright, & M.E. Ward. (1989). *Educating Special Learners.* (3d ed.), p. 182. Belmont, Calif. Wadsworth Publishing Co.

with a computer, can be used by pupils with various disabilities and pupils who are not disabled.

As Figure 3-7 shows, the teacher in a mainstream classroom can expect to find pupils from all seven handicapping conditions and from a variety of levels of disability within each category. For example, pupils who have a learning disability classified as mild or moderate will be present. However, only at level 6 or 7 would we routinely expect both mild and moderate classifications of behavioral disorders. The selection and use of computer hardware for students with special needs present a series of unique challenges. Initially the professionals must face the vexing issue of what to select. Is the selection based on numbers of students to be served, or on the severity of difficulty for the learner? How much transfer can be expected from one activity or task to another? Is this a stand-alone unit or can it be combined with others to form some sort of a unified support system?

The computer is not by its nature particularly adaptive to the needs of persons with disabling conditions. The basic keyboard requires that the user be able not only to strike the keys but also to read or "see" the keys. Additionally, the visual image appearing on the screen must be seen and interpreted to determine the appropriate procedure to follow.

Note that severity of disability does not always correlate with residential placement. For example, a child with a severe vision impairment should be served in the regular classroom, while a child with profound retardation may need to be schooled in a residential setting. Placement depends on what a multi-disciplinary team deems appropriate to meet student needs, always considering the mandate that learners with special needs should be with nondisabled peers as much as possible. Note, too, that placement depends on how a student functions.

Take two learners with severe vision impairments, Sam and Gerry. Sam has excellent orientation and mobility skills. He uses braille with ease and functions on a fourth-grade level. Sam could easily be placed in the fourth grade. Gerry, on the other hand, has had no training in orientation and mobility. He needs to use braille but has had no access to a teacher because he slipped through the "child-find" network and his parents sought no early intervention for him. He might be appropriately placed in a residential or self-contained classroom setting until his skill level is raised so that he can function comfortably in the mainstream.

Hardware/Pupil Placement

One of the critical factors necessary for determining the placement of hardware deals with the interpretation of and the development of each student's IEP. The current Individuals with Disabilities Education Act states that if the IEP calls for a student to have a particular type of hardware or assistive device (or a particular book or piece of software) that the item *follows* the student and is his or hers for the duration of the educational experience. To the extent that it is educationally feasible to share anything, the unit cost of providing services to all students decreases if more students can be served by an individual item. This is "economically smart" and should always be considered an option open to the faculty and administration of any school site, assuming the intent of PL 94-142 is not compromised. Additionally, a statement of needed transition services at no later than 16 years of age (14 years if appropriate) must be added to the school-generated IEP.

Software for Special Education

When working with students with special needs many issues must be addressed before the determination of the appropriateness of a specific software package can be made. The major item before the teacher is whether the software being considered maintains the established learning sequence for the particular student. Additionally, the teacher or other professional must be certain that concerns relative to the student's specific disability are addressed.

Figure 3-8 shows the rather simple diagram of how the student interacts with the computer in a rather direct, in/out flow. Figure 3-9 shows the student with special needs and the relationship between the learner and assistive devices and the learner and assistive software. Specific illustrations and more discussion of assistive devices appear in Chapter 6 and 7, while software is discussed in Chapter 5.

Laboratory or Individual Placement

The issue of having in-school computer labs versus the disbursement of hardware to individual teacher sites is a continuing and important consideration for persons charged with the delivery of services to students with special needs. On the

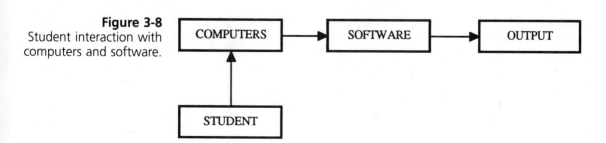

Figure 3-8
Student interaction with computers and software.

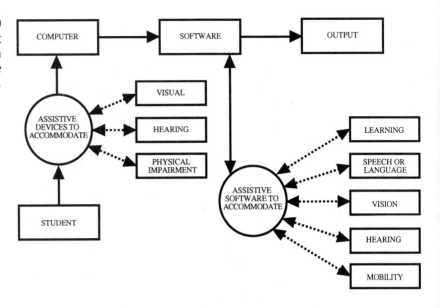

Figure 3-9
Special needs student interaction with computer and assistive devices/software.

one hand, the idea of a lab with numerous machines under the supervision of a single instructor or a team of instructors and aides is appealing from a management and logistical standpoint. After all, the teacher(s) can have absolute control of the situation and the teaching activities and support services are monitored in a clear, easily controlled manner. Coupled with the opportunity to network much of the software and monitor performance visually or from a single workstation is appealing to many teachers, administrators, and computer personnel.

The "other school of thought" believes that the disbursement of hardware (and, to a more limited degree, software) to individual teacher or student stations is the best way to effect good instruction and to deliver appropriate instruction to the learner—especially the learner with special needs. Many experts argue that an individual copy of a good word-processing package, a spreadsheet program, and a database-management program is the major set of software needed by the teacher to facilitate the learning of most students with special needs. The addition of a program like Print Shop (a program that facilitates preparation of student materials such as maps, crossword puzzles, etc.) is often a welcome addition to the base software set. These same teachers and administrators say the remainder of the software collection for a school or site could then be collected in one location and retrieved on an as-needed basis and shared by the many users in the building. As an individual piece of software became more widely used by a specific teacher or student, more copies would need to be added. This approach can facilitate a cost saving, reduce duplication of effort, and prevent "hoarding" of programs (Brownell, 1992).

Clearly, the philosophy of instruction and instructional organization are involved in such decisions. On the one hand, the use of computer labs for large group instruction has a long, profitable history in schools and colleges. The ability to gather equipment in one place, the opportunity to share hardware and such auxiliary devices as printers and scanners, the convenience of storage of consumable supplies, and the securing of such areas make the lab a desirable option from many perspectives.

On the other hand, advocates of disbursement believe there is a need to have the hardware and software *with* the student where he or she is. They provide such a powerful argument that it cannot be overlooked. These persons believe the movement of students with special needs to a specific location (i.e., the computer lab) is not only an unsound educational process, but tends to further fragment the very reason for having a mainstreamed program. The isolation factor is increased dramatically and the integration of the student with the instructional program is further fragmented.

The authors believe that, when appropriate, local site or district computer personnel should be actively involved in the issues of hardware and software selection and procurement. However, in the area of serving the needs of students with special needs, there are a number of vital considerations.

First, the site or system consultant is unlikely to have much firsthand knowledge of the special needs of special learners. Many consultants have been selected because of their background with software in math, science, or reading. The opportunities to interact with or have a major knowledge of broad-based issues important to students with special needs may be limited. Second, the possible conflicts airing between group instruction (e.g., computer labs) and the individual needs of a small number of students can pose a possible dilemma related to determining the most efficient/effective use of limited resources for the *most* students.

Finally—and perhaps of most importance—the basic integration of instructional materials appropriate for students with disabilities and the use of assistive devices/computers to create a least restrictive learning environment are not tasks for which a large number of persons are well equipped.

Testing Issues

In the interest of equity in assessment, certain concerns for testing are evident. Five categories generally are recognized for the purposes of providing test accommodations: learning disability, hearing impairment, visual impairment, physical disability, and mental disorders (Testing Persons with Disabilities: A Report for ETS Programs and Their Constituents, ETS, Princeton, N.J., 1990).

The legal basis for all test accommodation is found in Section 504 of the Rehabilitation Act of 1973, which makes discrimination on the basis of handicap in any program receiving federal assistance illegal. Section 504 does *not* require that all disabled individuals receive test accommodations. Rather, the law is directed toward those disabilities that negatively affect test performance but not criterion performance. That is, if the intended skill or ability would be measured less accurately for the disabled examinee than for the nondisabled examinee, then test accommodations are indicated. For academic tests, a variety of accommodations might be deemed appropriate.

Among the special accommodations that test sponsors are encouraged to offer are alternative test versions, assistive personnel, assistive devices, separate testing locations, and extra time. The provision of ancillary test materials in alternate formats and special scoring services comparable to those available to nondisabled examinees should also be encouraged. Recent research indicates that scores from special administrations of tests are largely comparable in meaning to those from standard administrations (though disability groups do not always receive average scores similar to the nondisabled population).

Section 504, then, does not require that every person with a disability be given an accommodation. Rather, the basis for accommodation appears to be whether the disability produces a dysfunction in a domain that would negatively affect test but *not* criterion performance (e.g., the examinee experiences difficulty reading the instructions for a performance test that does not require reading). The main objective is to provide an equally accurate assessment of both disabled and nondisabled examinees in terms of the skill or ability the test is intended to measure.

The appropriateness of test accommodations needs to be carefully considered. Whereas it is appropriate to offer accommodations designed to minimize the influence of irrelevant factors (of which the disability may or may not be one), it is generally inappropriate to provide accommodations when similar modifications are not allowed in regular school programs. Accommodations usually allowed in school programs include extra time and rest periods, the use of a sign language interpretation or a reader, and such format translations as braille, cassette, or large type since each of these accommodations is designed to minimize a particular type of irrelevant influence; the use of these accommodations is justified from Standards for Educational and Psychological, 1985.

Alternative Test Versions

Tests may be made available in alternate formats, including braille, cassette, or large type. Generally, test forms selected for presentation in these formats are developed in such a way that the same item content can be represented in both standard and alternate versions. Alternative ways to record answers to test questions may also be offered. The machine-scoreable answer sheet that accompanies many standardized tests can be replaced by marking answers in the test booklet itself, by using a large-type answer sheet, by using a typewriter to record the answers on a separate sheet, or by sorting cards into piles to indicate T/F or multiple-choice answers.

Assistive Personnel

Assistive personnel include those who read print tests to persons who have a vision impairment or a learning disability, record answers for candidates with vision or physical disabilities, or translate test instructions into signs for people who have a hearing impairment.

Assistive Devices

Assistive devices such as an Optacon, Visualtek, braille notetaker, typewriter, or talking calculator may sometimes be used to aid the examinee in reading questions, figuring, or recording responses.

Separate Testing Locations

Tests that are routinely group-administered are often offered to individuals with disabilities in a one-to-one administration. Separate testing locations make possible special accommodations that might be disturbing to other test-takers (e.g., the use of a reader or a cassette version of a test). Testing is also provided in special locations, such as an examinee's home or hospital room.

Extra Time

Most standardized tests are administered within specific time limits. Time limits are imposed as an administrative convenience or because speed is an aspect of what the test is intended to measure. Extra time may be offered for completing the test or for rest periods between timed test sections. The provision of extra time is especially important when special test formats are used. For example, braille takes longer to read than print. Similarly, moving back and forth between a question and a reading passage is more time-consuming with cassette than with printed text. Because of visual or motor impairments, some examinees may need more time to mark answer sheets. Some may need longer or additional rest periods.

Summary

This chapter has concentrated on computers and learning with special emphasis on the way computers and the teacher can unite to meet learner goals. Instructional delivery formats and pupil placement are discussed. Concerns about how the computer facilitates the improvement of instruction and how the computer can be integrated into the classroom are discussed. The relationship between the computer and its effectiveness as an instructional tool is noted. Levels of computer usage dealing with enhancing existing materials and approaches, using software, adapting existing software, and creating original software are discussed. Instructional delivery formats including cooperative learning, individualistic learning, and competitive learning are discussed, as are the concepts of service delivery, hardware placement, and software for special education. Finally, issues of computer labs versus individual placement and testing issues are addressed.

References

Brownell, G. (1992). *Computers and teaching* (2nd ed.). (pp. 494–496). St. Paul, MN: West Publishing Company.

Dick, W., & Carey, L. (1978). *The systematic design of instruction.* Glenview, IL: Scott, Foresman and Company.

Johnson, D. W., & Johnson, R. T. (1991). *Learning together and alone: Cooperative, competitive and individualistic learning* (3rd ed.). Englewood Cliffs, NJ: Prentice-Hall.

Kagan, S. (1989, December). The structural approach to cooperative learning. *Educational Leadership,* 12–15.

Kaplan-Neher, A. (1992, February–March). Using computers in instruction. *Syllabus, 21,* 12–15.

Office of Corporate Quality Assurance and ETS Committee on People with Disabilities. (1990). *Testing persons with disabilities: A report for ETS programs and their constituents.* Princeton, NJ: Educational Testing Service.

Simon, H. A., & Feigenbaum, E. A. (1964). An information-processing theory of verbal learning. *Journal of Verbal Learning and Verbal Behavior, 3,* 385–396.

Sutton, R. E. (1991). Equity and computers in the schools: A decade of research. *Review of Educational Research, 61,* 475–503.

Tateyama-Sniezek, K. M. (1990). Cooperative learning: Does it improve the academic achievement of students with handicaps? *Exceptional Children, 56,* 426–437.

Testing people who have handicapping conditions. (1985). *Standards for educational and psychological testing* (pp. 77–80). Washington, DC: American Psychological Association.

Watkins, B. T. (1991, September 4). The electronic classroom. *Chronicle of Higher Education,* A26–A28.

Watson, J. (1991–1992). Cooperative learning and computers: One way to address student differences. *Computing Teacher Conference Issue,* 5–8.

Computer Hardware

Objectives

After reading this chapter, you should be able to:

- List and describe the major components of a microcomputer system.
- Describe the function of the various devices that comprise a computer system.
- Discuss the price/performance relationship in selecting computers.
- Describe the function and use of networks in support of instruction.
- Discuss possible future trends in computer hardware and its relation to use of adaptive devices.

Much of the material presented in previous chapters has dealt with the major issues of disabilities and how persons in schools deal with them. Definitions of various disabilities and the interrelationships between/among them have been discussed. Material relating to learners with special needs and those who teach them has spoken to how learners are alike and how they are different. Now our emphasis will shift to those nonhuman facilitators of learning—computer hardware and software.

While there are literally hundreds if not thousands of electronic devices that students with special needs can use, the basic computer system that supports such applications needs to be described first. Many but not all of the assistive devices illustrated and discussed in this text are "controlled" through the use of a microcomputer. In Appendix D we provide a section on the basics of computers. This chapter will provide more detail and describe the hardware elements of the computer system.

A Bit of History

Much computer development over the past several years has resulted from a long history of activity—successes and failures—undertaken by a number of persons with creative ideas and the will to translate those ideas into "things" that can be utilized for various tasks or for specific applications.

The history of computing is filled with the names of persons whose contributions to the field may seem almost trivial. But when their contributions are examined in detail we realize that these pioneers provided crucial links that brought an invention or a process from the conceptual stage, to the developmental stage, to the production stage, to the use stage.

The development of the computer as a representative of today's technology has been broad and detailed, yet short and punctuated with spectacular successes. Time lines, while meaningless in some ways, do show gradual change against some norm.

A Long Time Ago

Probably the earliest counting or computational device was the abacus. Developed by the Chinese more than 4,500 years ago, this bead-strung device was useful in dealing with subtraction and addition problems. The abacus, as a method of computation, survived as "state of the art" until the 1600s, when John Napier developed a table of numbers—basically a primitive slide rule—which aided in division and multiplication problems. This innovation was called Napier's Rods.

Automated Computational Materials

In the mid-1600s Blaise Pascal developed a gear-operated machine capable of adding and "understanding." The ability of this machine to "carry forward" from

63

one gear to the next proved to be what was really the first mechanical calculator. Gottfried Leibniz improved Pascal's machine in the late 1600s by changing its design so that the machine could multiply, divide, and do square roots.

Charles Babbage was the first person to propose the concept of what is now the modern computer. His basic idea was to build a machine that would calculate squares, logs, and other number functions quickly and accurately. During the mid-1880s Babbage designed and partially built a differential engine that would perform such functions. He later designed and built the workable, newer version that we know as the analytical engine.

Ada Byron (Countess of Lovelace) became interested in the efforts of Babbage and became his partner in later efforts at refinement of the analytical engine. She is credited with introducing the concept of binary rather than decimal storage. Additionally her work with what we call program loops allowed calculations to be performed with much less effort. Thus, she became the first computer programmer.

Many other persons contributed pieces or ideas to computing and computer development. Detailed discussions are beyond the scope of this book, but people such as Jacquard and his loom and Levillian Burrough and his commercially successful adding machines are examples of the scores of such persons who deserve mention. The Computer Museum in Boston, local libraries, hardware vendors, and other sources contain the names and contributions of many other figures in the history of computing.

Modern Computing

In a more recent period, such people as Herman Hollerith (who developed the punched card tabulator and was also one of the founders of IBM), John Mauchly and J. Presper Eckert (inventors of the ENIAC), John von Neumann (who introduced the stored program concept), and Tom Watson (a major force behind the growth of IBM) have made lasting contributions to computing.

Developmental Time Lines

While the purpose of this text is not to train experts in computer history or development, there is a series of major events in the recent history of computers and related areas that are of importance to even the most casual user. (Appendix E is a chart showing key events in computer development paired with key events in the history of special education.)

To illustrate the relatively short history of the computer and the even shorter time of use of computers in education, Appendix E shows the steps in the development of computers. The advance that made the use of computers in education feasible was the development of the integrated circuit—"the computer on a chip." The first chip to appear was the Intel 4004 chip in 1971; the more complex VLSI (very large-scale integrated) chips appeared later in the IBM PC. In 1976 the Apple I computer board was designed by Steven Jobs and Steve Wozniak, leading to the first general usage in schools. IBM and other companies began to produce hardware for the educational market at an ever-increasing rate.

The "marriage" of computers to special needs devices has occurred over a period of years and has spawned the development of a major market in technology —both hardware and software. A detailed discussion of several such devices and their computer "hosts" appears in Chapters 6 and 7.

Computers

A computer is an electronic device capable of arithmetic and logic (tests and decisions) operations that are directed by stored sets of instructions. Computer systems perform these basic information-processing functions: input information, process information, store information, and output information.

For this text it is sufficient to note that most computer manufacturers classify computers into four size groupings:

1. **Supercomputer**—Any of the group of computers that have the fastest processing speeds available at a given time for solving scientific or engineering calculations (e.g., a Cray computer can do millions of calculations per second).

2. **Mainframe**—A large computer, in particular one to which other computers can be connected so that they can share facilities the mainframe provides. For example, a System/370 computing system allows personal computers to be attached so that they can upload (pull information from the mainframe) and download (give information to the mainframe) programs and data.

3. **Minicomputer**—An intermediate-size computer that can perform the same kinds of applications as a mainframe but has less storage capacity, processing power, and speed than a mainframe.

4. **Microcomputer**—A small computer that includes one or more input/output units and sufficient memory to execute instructions (e.g., a personal computer). The essential components of a microcomputer are often contained within a single enclosure.

The majority of the instructional and administrative support applications discussed in this text are those used with a microcomputer. However, the school district or local schools may have mainframe applications, generally in the areas of administrative and instructional support. For example, accounting and payroll applications for the district as well as test scoring and analysis for individual students, classrooms, schools, and districts are likely to be performed on a mainframe. Many other applications—both system-wide and state-wide—may require the use of a mainframe computer, but as the networking of PCs becomes more common these mainframe functions may be shifted to a network of some type.

While the above applications are noteworthy and extremely important to learners, teachers, and administrators, the basic day-to-day concerns of teachers of students with special needs key on the ability to provide effective, efficient, direct instructional services. Because of the nature of students with special needs, standard microcomputer applications are likely to be insufficient for meeting their needs. Some persons with disabilities may have major difficulty with keyboard access; others may have major problems with display images or trouble depressing multiple keys.

Major Computer Components

Regardless of size computers are composed of four major components. Figure 4-1 provides an illustration of these in graphic form. These are:

1. Input devices
2. Output devices
3. Central processing unit (CPU)
4. External memory (auxiliary storage)

Figure 4-1
Graphic view of major computer components.

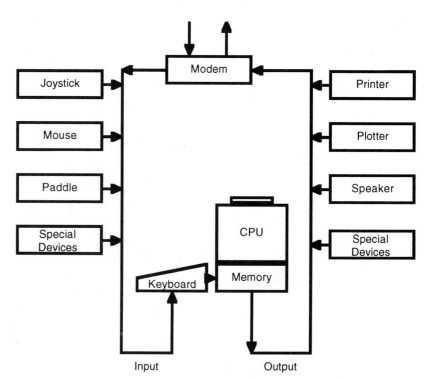

Figure 4-2
Phases/stages of
integration of
microcomputers into the
K-12 classroom.

Phase	Name	Time Period
First	Experiment	1960s
Second	Popularization	Late 1970s
	Familiarization	1974–1984
Third	Transition	Mid-1980s
	Maturation	1984–1986
Fourth	Infusion	Late 1980s
Fifth	Integration	Future

Microcomputers

For most applications references to the computer in this book are to the microcomputer that is so common in today's schools, businesses, government agencies, and homes. Many schools—public, private, and parochial—have these machines available for faculty and student use. Teachers' and school administrators' exposure to computers and applications ranges from limited to major. The phases/stages of integration of the microcomputer into the K–12 classroom are shown in Figure 4-2. Discussion of teacher and administrator and instructional support training areas appears in Chapter 2, and are important elements in the integration of the computer into the classroom and into the total school program.

Developments in computer hardware and software continue at a rapid rate. Also, development of adaptive hardware and the software to support it continues to increase. New hardware items, laptops, palmtops, hand-held microcomputers, and the even newer personal organizers will have an impact on the education of the student with special needs, but currently we do not know what this impact will be.

Figure 4-3 shows the number of units in thousands shipped and the value of those units in millions of dollars during 1990 and 1991. The "big three"—IBM, Apple, and Compaq—remain at the top, but systems like Gateway 2000 and Dell have shown substantial increases. However, this trend would need to be broad-based and long-term for these companies to become major players in the educational market. Cost considerations drive purchases of school computers. The

Figure 4-3
Computer scale
revenues and units
shipped for 1991 and
1990.

Rank	Company	1991 ($ millions)	1991 Units (Thousands)	1990 ($ millions)	1990 Units (Thousands)
1.	IBM	*3,384	1,200	*3,760	1,200
2.	Apple Computer	2,450	1,020	2,230	618
3.	Compaq Computer	1,546	411	1,550	411
4.	Tandy Corporation	700	350	680	340
5.	Gateway 2000	635	250	275	104
6.	Toshiba Corporation	625	250	500	200
7.	NCR Corporation	609	243	684	274
8.	Dell Computer Corp.	595	270	382	153
9.	Unisys Corporation	560	200	567	227
10.	NEC Corporation	480	175	300	125

*Datamation, April 1992

introduction of lower-price clones has reduced the per unit costs; this pressure will continue at least for the short term.

While the day-to-day practical "need to know" value of this information for teachers may be questionable, we note it because the smaller the number of companies involved in hardware and software sales to schools the higher the costs. There would also be little incentive to develop software for small groups (e.g., students with disabilities comprise a small percent of total school populations).

While the use of the information in Figure 4-3 is of a limited nature, it does illustrate the short time the computer has had major impact on the instruction of children, most especially students with special needs. The ideas of infusion (simply placing a machine on site) and integration (making use of the machine in myriad ways) of the computer as a viable instructional tool are really in their infancy.

The microcomputer is designed for individual users (though some research supports the idea that two to three students working together on a computer is a better tactic than individual use) which can provide special learning opportunities for teachers and students. A typical microcomputer system (Figure 4-1) includes at least the following components (very much like those noted before):

- CPU—the microcomputer itself
- Keyboard (and probably a mouse)
- Monitor
- Disk drive(s)
- Printer

It is important for faculty, students, and staff to have a working knowledge of how each element of the system functions.

The major component of any system, the CPU, includes the control unit, the arithmetic/logic unit, and the main memory. The control unit manages the activities performed in the CPU. Monitoring, routing, and analyzing instructions and functions are performed by the control unit. The arithmetic/logic unit processes information and data provided through the input devices and provides for the direction of the control unit. It is in this portion of the computer that actual "number crunching" takes place. Remember that input for processing may be in the form of numbers, letters, special characters, sounds, electronic impulses, or a myriad of other forms/sources. Main memory is where data/information is stored before and after analyses.

DEFINITION: Central Processing Unit (CPU)

The component of a computer system with the circuitry to control the interpretation and execution of instructions. The CPU includes the arithmetic/logic and control sections. Synonymous with *central processor* and *mainframe.*

The CPU contains the electronics that actually perform the processing of a computer. The CPU includes the arithmetic/logic and control sections. "CPU" is also used to refer to the central processor and mainframe.

Memory

Memory is of two types: read only memory (ROM) and random access memory (RAM). It is sufficient for our use to consider ROM as permanent storage and RAM as temporary storage. External memory (more RAM) is often added to machines to extend the functions performed. These are stand-alone units and are available in blocks (really just like adding another floor to a building or another row of chairs to an auditorium). (Appendix D on Computer Basics discusses the differences in storage and memory and notes the use of floppy disks as storage devices.)

ROM/RAM. The main memory, or what is often called internal storage, includes permanent memory and temporary memory. The permanent memory is called ROM and the temporary memory is called RAM.

ROM includes information programmed into any computer at the manufacturing stage, including some languages. Large machines often use a machine language understood only by system personnel, while microcomputers use a more simple language like BASIC. Additionally, programs are included that translate that language into the digits understood by the computer. Information in ROM cannot be changed or altered.

RAM, on the other hand, serves as the workplace for the computer. When information is brought into the computer memory, and used (e.g., you write a paragraph), it is then lost when the machine is turned off (unless you save it) or if new material is written over that set. RAM also provides workspace for the user when programming or providing instructions for a software package. Remember that RAM information varies from application to application and is lost when the machine is disconnected or turned off. ROM remains the same with or without power to the machine.

DEFINITION: Optical Disc

A groveless disc on which digital data stored as text, sounds, or pictures are stored as tiny pits in the surface. The disc is read or replayed by a laser beam scanning the surface.

CD ROM. "Emerging" technologies associated with computers and computer-related assistive devices are in such a growth curve that to project costs or new applications is like trying to predict the weather six months in advance. A classic example of an emerging technology is the optical disc. Perhaps of equal importance is some of the recently introduced applications for the compact disc-read only memory (CD ROM). While generally limited to storing large amounts of data, the number of potential applications is unparalled, especially in database problems. CD ROMs contain much more information than common silicon ROM chips. A single CD ROM can hold up to 650 megabytes—more than enough room for an entire encyclopedia of information. CD ROMs can be changed like floppy disks. They are often cross-indexed so thoroughly that the indexing takes up more of the available space on a disc than the information itself. HyperText may play a part in solving this problem. HyperCard, a software package, is an example of HyperText and is described in the software chapter.

DEFINITION: CD ROM

High-capacity read-only memory in the form of an optically read compact disc.

Modems

Modems are used for transmitting and receiving data over telephone lines. These devices perform the signal conversions required to link microcomputers with telephone systems. The term *modem* is derived from the two functions a modem performs: modulation and demodulation. Modulation is the conversion of computer digital signals into telephone analog signals; demodulation is the reverse procedure. Computers need digital signals, while telephone lines may use analog signals.

DEFINITION: Analog-to-Digital Converter

A mechanical or electrical device that changes continuous analog (e.g., temperature readings) to discrete digital numbers (e.g., whole numbers).

The speed at which data transmission occurs is known as the "baud rate." A model rated at 1200 baud is capable of sending data at about 1,200 bits per second. Inexpensive modems range in speed from 300 baud to 2400 baud. Moderately priced modems have speeds up to 4800 baud. Expensive modems range upward to 9600 and even 19,200 baud. A typical 300-baud modem transmits 37 characters per second; a 2400-baud modem transmits 300 characters per second. A message that takes 2 hours to transmit at 300 baud can be transmitted in about

15 minutes at 2400 baud. The faster 9600 baud modems are becoming more commonly used.

There is a cost trade-off involved in selecting baud rate. The modems that allow faster transmission are more expensive, but the cost of using telephone lines is also expensive and determined by the length of the call. Faster transmission may save money in the long run. The price of modems begins at $50 and ranges to several hundred dollars, depending on speed and features.

Modems are either internal or external. Internal modems are built into or inserted into a microcomputer's expansion slots. External modems are connected to the computer by cable. In either case, the modem is connected to a telephone line for transmission and reception.

Communications software is required to use a modem. This software provides an interface between the data being transmitted or received and the modem. In the simplest case, the communications software allows the user to utilize the microcomputer as a terminal for entering responses to another remote computer or to display text from a remote computer on the user's monitor.

Networking

Generally, telecommunications software allows a microcomputer to access other computing resources to obtain information, update files, or send messages. Telecommunications is done via telephone lines, microwave relay, satellite transmission, or local area networks (LANs) and wide area networks (WANs). (See section on networks in this chapter.)

Networking is a rapidly growing type of instructional opportunity for the special needs learner that holds great promise for the future. For example, some states have provided Internet Access for all teachers in the state. Other groups such as the National Geographic Society have provided opportunities for both national and international exchange of information for students working on projects involving environmental education.

Input Devices

Typewriter-like keyboards are the most typical input devices. However, especially for students with special needs, a variety of input devices allowing for use of touch, sound, and other activation modes are used with computers. Input also may be from scanning devices and other light- or sound-sensitive hardware items. Examples of special input devices appear in the chapters on assistive devices. (See Chapters 6 and 8.)

Keyboard. A keyboard is a group of marked levers operated by the fingers (or some assistive device) for the purpose of recording characters. Most keyboards have the appearance of a typewriter, with letters, numbers, and special characters. Most keyboards in use today also have function keys, which are used to communicate specific things to the computer. For example, the F7 key on a standard IBM computer keyboard is used with *WordPerfect* (a word-processing program) to cause the software program to print processed information (use Shift-F7). Other special keys such as [Delete], [Return], and [Enter] and the control keys of [←], [→], [↑], and [↓] cause instructions or data to be entered and sent to the microprocessor.

Alternative Input Methods. While a keyboard is the most commonly used method of providing input to a microcomputer, an individual with a motor control impairment may not be able to use a keyboard effectively. Adaptations allow the computer to accept characters or commands coming from the alternative input methods just as if they were coming from the computer's standard keyboard.

When choosing an alternative method for computer input, one should make sure that it will work with all software applications to be used, such as word-processing programs and database programs. One input method uses a *switch* to enter the same data that would have been keyed. A wide variety of switches are activated by almost any motion of any part of the body. A switch adapts to the voluntary actions that the user can reliably control. For example, a switch may be turned "on" or "off" by sipping and puffing on a tube, wrinkling the eyebrows, or making contact with a metal plate. A switch interface, which can be a software program or hardware device, acts as the link between the switch and the computer.

Figure 4-5
Switch-For Use by students with physical disabilities. *Courtesy of International Business Machines Corporation.*

A modern technique for operating a computer is *scanning*. The user selects the desired characters or word from the computer display or a separate panel. With scanning, a cursor or highlighted area moves repeatedly from one character (or group of characters) to the next. With several activations, the selection is entered into the computer as if it had been typed at the keyboard.

DEFINITION: Scanner

A device that examines a spatial pattern one part after another, and generates analog or digital signals corresponding to the pattern. Scanners are often used in mark sensing, pattern recognition, or character recognition.

Scanners have a variety of uses for the special needs learner (see Figure 6-12). One specific illustration allows scanners to send text to speech synthesizers and to store for later use. Control units or switches also may be strategically placed for ease of use by the visually disabled (Sensory Access Foundation). Reading machines such as the 1993 Kurzweil Reading Edge produced by Xerox, Imaging Systems (XIS), and the Arkenstone Reading machine (An Open Book) use optical character recognition (OCR) software. This software makes the best guess as to what the correct word should be and must also guess at correct pronunciation.

With a *direct selection* method, the user "points to" the target items through a single action such as eye gaze, head pointer, or light beam. The characters selected may be displayed on the computer terminal or on a separate panel.

An alternative input method by which a computer accepts a spoken command is *voice recognition*. A computer can only do this if it has a previously stored voice pattern to compare with the incoming sound. With some voice recognition systems, the person using the system must first train the computer by repeating the key word or phrase several times into the microphone attached to the computer. The computer saves this as a voice pattern. To use a voice recognition system successfully, an individual should be able to reproduce the same speech patterns that were used when the system was set up; that is, the user needs to speak the same way every time. When the computer receives voice commands for input to the system, it matches these against the stored voice patterns and executes the keystrokes that were set up for that command. Four other types of input devices are:

Joy stick—in computer graphics, a lever that can pivot in all directions and that is used as a locator device

Paddle—a device used in computer games to control the position of a cursor by moving a lever

Tablet—a special flat surface with a mechanism for indicating positions thereon, normally used as a locator

Reader—a device that converts information in one form of storage to information in another form of storage

Output Devices

The two primary output devices are the display screen of the monitor and the printer. Virtually all computer-linked machines have a visual output (screen) while most allow for hard copy (printer) output. Again, other devices using sound, sight, or other electronic responses are in wide use for instructional activities for students with special needs.

Monitor. A keyboard is commonly attached to a television-like device called a monitor (the device typically has no channel selector). The monitor allows for a visual display of both input and output. Sizes range from about 12 to 14 inches diagonally. Monitor size is much smaller on laptop and most portable computers. Color monitors are popular. They are more expensive, but almost essential in a teaching situation where "fine" differentiations are needed or graphics are a major feature.

Printers. These are typewriter-like devices that allow for the production of hard copy (paper) for output purposes. The printers commonly used in school settings are either dot matrix or laser, with the former being predominant. Laser printers that produce an excellent quality print are becoming more and more affordable for schools and administrative offices. The value of printers basically is based on speed. Speed is measured in output of characters per second or pages per minute. Many higher-quality printers have control over such functions as font size (the size of the print), forward and reverse paper scrolling, and proportional spacing. Color is also an option on some printers.

Plotters. One device that produces graphic output in permanent form is the plotter. Directed by signals from the computer, the plotter moves a pen across a piece of paper. A plotter equipped with more than one pen can produce multi-color graphic output. The flat-bed plotter holds a sheet of paper on a flat surface; it then moves a pen across the sheet to form images. With a drum plotter, the paper is wound around a drum; the paper's rotation and pen movement are computer-coordinated to produce the appropriate image. With both types, two- or three-dimensional graphics can be created.

Plotters are high-quality, low-volume devices; they are unable to mass produce graphic outputs efficiently. High-volume output requires laser printers and special cameras.

Figure 4-6
Plotter. *Courtesy of Hewlett-Packard.*

Cost Factors

An important hardware selection consideration is always price. Issues of memory size, speed, and graphics capability are all important to the teacher and the user, but school business administrators often have one bottom line: cost! While costs of many other facets of education—salaries, benefits, consumable supplies, textbooks, and transportation—have mushroomed, the dollar bought remarkably more in computer technology in 1991 than in 1981. Figure 4-7 shows what a $2,000 expenditure bought in 1991 compared to 1981. As with most items, the

Figure 4-7
Personal computer
system. *Source:*
Electronic Learning,
February, 1992, p. 20.
Prepared by Isabelle
Bruder.

Average 1981 Personal Computer	Average 1991 Personal Computer
Stand-alone machine	Networkable machine
Memory: 4K to 64K	Memory: 640K to 8MB
Storage: cassette recorder	Storage: 360K to 1.2 gigabyte hard drive 16 to 16 million
Monitor: Mostly monochrome, except the RGB (red, green, blue) Apple II and Commodore 64	Monitor: Color
Graphics: Low resolution highly bit-mapped (fuzzy to the eye)	Graphics: high resolution
Sound: computer simulated	Sound: Audio input, stereo output
Operating speed: 1Mhz	Operating speed: 8 Mhz and up
Input: keyboard	Input: keyboard, mouse, trackball, other devices
Floppy disk drive: separate	Floppy disk drive: one or more built-in; CD-ROM drive

passage of time shows computing cost for any specific task to have fallen steadily. Computer power also has increased dramatically, but the ability to use *all* available power always lags behind due to the lack of appropriate software.

The same "bargain" prices hold for most hardware items when output and thruput (the amount of work that can be accomplished) is considered. Additionally, many areas of instruction can now be supported by hardware items (e.g.,

> ## DEFINITION: Plotter
>
> An output unit that presents data in the form of a two- or three-dimensional graphic representation.

videodisc) that were not available to the mass market only a few years ago. For example, in 1991 every school site (building) in the state of Florida had a videodisc player. The issue of availability of discs not withstanding, the appropriate usage is not always as easily determined, but the hardware cost per unit is a real value for our education dollar.

Networks

There is an "age-old" dilemma of whether to use computers in an individual classroom, in a laboratory setting, or in both. Physical arrangements and availability have substantial influence on how machines are arranged in local sites. The ability to have immediate, teacher-controlled access to the machines (laboratory setting) is balanced against the ability to have a large number of programs used simultaneously or one program used by a large number of students. Opportunities for effective and efficient instruction exist in any arrangement.

The ability for "networking" available at local school sites is the ability to distribute the same program or multiple programs to large numbers of people from a single source. For example, if all students are working on the same math program, then one copy of the math program—with the appropriate site license—can be loaded onto the network and presented to each terminal. Similarly, if pupils are working on a number of different programs (e.g., science, social studies, writing, math) then the individual programs can be selected from a file server and accessed individually by each student at a terminal. The network capability allows a teacher/observer to monitor the classroom and to be available when any individual has a question. In a similar way a non-network system can work with individual pieces of software one student at a time. If more than one student is working on a particular program, however, then a copy must be purchased for each machine or, in the event a site license has been obtained, the program must be loaded onto each machine. After loading, the disk may be removed and moved to another machine. In rare instances the program disks may need to be resident (or remain) in the machine; some software items require a disk for each machine. In most instances the purchase of one copy of a program does *not* provide the school system with the proper authority to have that program loaded onto more than one machine. A separate license must be obtained for that function. (Site licenses in general and the ethics and legal issues involved in copying are addressed in Chapter 5.)

A LAN is a system of computers and associated peripherals such as printer or scanner that are physically connected by cable within one department, building, or group of buildings. WANs connect computers in various geographic locations using the types of connections noted above. Many networks are managed through the use of a dedicated computer called a file server. Networking allows for greater control of what is distributed to students through the teacher's ability to monitor what goes out from the file server. This may raise questions about the security of information stored and available to any (or all) of the workstations, however. The need to purchase a site license for use of programs may also be a factor. The key to arrangement (while briefly discussed here) is the delivery of services to the special needs learner. The effective teacher can use varied hardware configurations and can influence future decisions by his or her decisions concerning hardware usage.

One of the truly useful as well as innovative activities utilizing an out-of-building network is currently operated by the Harvard University Graduate School of Education. This network links approximately thirty-five of the school's graduates who have just started teaching in middle and high schools across the country. From computers in their homes, these teachers can send messages about how their work is progressing, seek advice, and/or just have a link with persons experiencing many of the same problems of teaching. Basically a per-user-at-a-time system, the link provides for communications that in other situations would take hours or days for a response (i.e., the mail). More communications links (lines) are possible as is equipment to transmit images of worksheets or texts. Again, the prohibitive factor is cost.

All of this discussion illustrates that computer links are feasible and not technically difficult to establish. Most important, they are useful to the user (*Chronicles of Higher Education*, November 6, 1991).

Disaster Recovery Plan

Recovery of computer records that have been destroyed or severely damaged due to a natural (lightning) or man-made disaster (fire or vandalism) is a task most persons do not like to think about and for which few make contingency plans. While no one expects a disaster, they can and do occur. Most computer users have adopted a file backup plan (copying files into a disk that is stored away from the computer). They discipline themselves to prepare backup files on an orderly, regular basis and have the foresight to store the resulting information at a remote site (and in a fireproof, burglar-proof vault). Remember that the production of a copy and the subsequent *on-site* storage can result in both the original and the copy being destroyed. The need for both hard copy and electronic (probably disk file) backup can only be determined by local personnel. Site-based needs may require hard copy or some form of readable copy. Some sites are now routinely using some type of microfiche (sheets) or microfilm (rolls) reproduction. However, most school systems (especially local sites) cannot afford the costs of this type of backup protection. Most school systems should protect records as best they can with locked, fire-resistant cabinets and appropriate disk backup. A general rule of thumb is to routinely back up and protect files on a half-day or daily basis and to make immediate backup of initial data or files.

Service Agreements

With all computers comes the need to provide appropriate maintenance and service support for the hardware. Regardless of how careful students, faculty, and staff are any hardware will at some time require service and repair. Basically, the school site and/or system should consider a variety of service contract options. Clearly, these options are tied to a price, with speed and location of reference (i.e., 24 hours at your site) a direct cost consideration. The ability to take the equipment to the repair location and to have the flexibility of some time delay are to the advantage of the user. Most maintenance agreements of this type allow for unlimited calls but at a relatively high cost. There is a major gamble, but one taken by many schools, when hardware is repaired on a per call basis. This is an expensive option on a given call, but if the number of calls is low, the user will save money. One note of caution: most on-site maintenance arrangements provide for periodic cleaning and preventive maintenance (vacuuming, etc.) by the seller that will not occur if no contract is in place. This level of maintenance needs to be implemented by the local site administrator to prevent avoidable breakdowns.

Summary

This chapter has presented material on the basic elements of computer systems used both to facilitate the use of adaptive devices and as stand-alone support systems for instruction, support service, and administration relative to special needs students. Many professionals have a basic knowledge of computers, but a brief refresher is good and if the information level is weaker, this chapter provides a way to tie the material together.

However, the larger issue—and one that is really paramount to the focus/use of this chapter—is the need to view the computer as an ally for providing the best possible educational opportunity for pupils. The computer as an instructional aid or as a "driver" for the adaptive devices noted in the next chapter is the key to the future success of efforts supported in this text. Much of the development of the computer is in the future. The future growth in both computers and adaptive devices is extremely promising. Costs are low and potential is up! The rapid development of hardware items means an increasing ability to provide a vast array of learning opportunities for the student and instructional opportunities for the faculty member. Development is a mixed blessing since increased costs are inevitably an outgrowth of development. Development also contributes to real or perceived obsolescence of in-place hardware. Planning for new hardware and the use of existing hardware are key points in effectively meeting the demands of the influx of new equipment.

References

Nicklin, J. (1991, November 6). For newly hired school teachers, an electronic lifeline. *Chronicles of Higher Education*, A24–A27.

Software

Objectives

After reading this chapter, you should be able to:

- Define key software terms: programming language, operating system, HyperMedia, LAN.
- Describe the function of software packages relative to instructional improvement for students with disabilities.
- Discuss the ethical use of software and the role of site licensing.
- Understand the evaluation process for selection and use of software packages.
- Discuss the legal issues associated with piracy of software.

Basic to the use of any computer system is the selection of appropriate software. Software is the set of programs chosen by the user to implement the instructional, administrative, or support function on the computer.

Software programs are a collection of coded statements written to communicate the ideas of the writer (programmer) in a way the computer understands. Computers generally use operating systems, which provide basic directions for the machine including checking to see that all components are operating and that memory is available for use. Additionally, most computers have a large program called a compiler, which allows coding or instructions written by the programmer to be understood by the machine. Programmers write programs using a set of instructions called a language. Languages vary in complexity and utility and often are geared to specific problem types. For example, a language called FORTRAN (Formula Translation) has always been a favorite of persons using computers to solve mathematic or engineering problems. On the other hand, COBOL (Common Business Oriented Language) has been a favorite of businesses. The most common language for microcomputers—while not necessarily the best—is BASIC (Beginners All Purpose Symbolic Instruction Code). The user of a microcomputer, whether a programmer or not, often has written a few lines of BASIC code as part of a literacy or basic applications course. (Appendix F contains a detailed discussion of programming languages that will be of interest to selected readers.)

In the past few years, software has become more and more a collection of pretested packages selected for use by teachers and other professionals. These packages are generally written by experts in a specific field whose main job is to develop software. Such software is technically good, usually written in a "user-friendly" format, and relatively inexpensive. Potential users must determine if the packaged software matches learner needs or the administrative needs of a particular program. For example, do the issues addressed in Package A address the learning schema for the grade and disability type for which it will be used?

Guidelines for software choice are as follows:

1. Software should encourage learning by doing by providing challenging, accomplishable tasks that motivate students.
2. Recognizing what to do is much easier than recalling what to do. Multiple choice should be used openly.
3. Most interesting questions have no agreed-on answers. Software should encourage students to explore a variety of possible answers.
4. Students respond to well-told stories. Software must have good stories to tell.
5. No computer should be allowed to be in control of the educational process. Students should have the power to determine what is coming next. (Schank, 1987–1988)

CAI/CMI

Instructional software is usually categorized as computer assisted instruction (CAI) or computer managed instruction (CMI). CAI connotes direct, one-to-one computer to student activity; it is extremely useful for drill and practice, simulation, and/or tutorial situations. CAI instruction is most often tailored to individual student's needs, and the assigned work is between the student and the teacher. Reports and records of student performance are provided by the software package, with the key being individualization of the activity. CMI is generally an application where the computer is used as a record keeper, manager, or prescriber of instructional activities. The machine logs the efforts of the student; it may then suggest certain activities or projects (including other software packages) for the individual student. The assignment may be a CAI lesson or a noncomputer-related assignment. The idea of managing the instructional efforts of many students is appealing, but requires a substantial planning effort by the teacher.

Much has been made of CAI, but many teachers are unable or unwilling to feel comfortable with existing programs for other than the most routine instructional efforts. The alternative is either to develop CAI programs or to use an authoring package to produce appropriate instructional items. The CAI option, while of interest, is an extremely labor-intensive effort and requires a level of computer knowledge not often possessed by the average classroom teacher. An article in the *Journal of Special Education* (MacArthur & Malouf, 1991) uses case studies to illustrate teachers' beliefs and knowledge about computing, the planning and decision-making processes, and the patterns of computer use in classrooms for special education teachers.

While not a matter of ability, the cost/return effort to create their own CAI is so small that most teachers opt for an alternative. The use of an authoring program is the most logical alternative available.

Authoring Packages

The more teachers and administrators become involved with computers, the more they want to have access to or to develop "good" software packages. The opportunity to find good software packages presents itself in many ways and in many places. The opportunity to "produce or write" special, site-specific software packages has never been appealing to a large number of educators. The main reason for this lack of desire is that the work is very demanding, exacting, and time-consuming. Good programs (or packages) take months or even years to write, test, rewrite, and market. Most teachers, even though they have the content knowledge, lack the specialized programming skills necessary to produce such code (program statements) and do not wish to devote a tremendous amount of time to learning a programming language or writing the programs. Even so, there is one tool (or usually a variable set of tools) now available to teachers that provides a workable compromise between writing from "scratch" or taking only what is commercially produced: the use of an *authoring language.*

Authoring systems and authoring languages provide a means for teachers and administrators to create CAI programs. In a very real sense, authoring packages allow microcomputer users to do programming without specialized knowledge.

The use of authoring systems requires no knowledge of programming. Typically, these packages are used to create microcomputer-based drill and practice materials. The author simply answers a series of prompts to provide the desired text and questions to be included in the materials. CAI programs created with such a system resemble one another in structure, relying heavily on a question/answer format. The author specifies a question and the correct answer, and anticipates wrong answers. When the student using the program enters an incorrect answer, the program brings up the response that was written for this choice. Unanticipated incorrect answers are handled with a set of answers or specific set of instructions.

Today's authoring systems have many desirable features. Many can accommodate the needs of individual students by either moving ahead for students who demonstrate mastery, or by looping backward for students who show that they need review. Student responses can be logged for later analysis, and students can stop a lesson one day and begin the next day where they left off.

Today's systems are also able to integrate videodiscs containing sound, slides, and motion sequences with instructional software.

Authoring languages provide more flexibility than authoring systems, but more training is needed to use them properly. With an authoring language, the user creates the framework of the program by using program statements in much the same way that programmers use a programming language. Because they are so flexible, these packages can be used for a wide variety of purposes.

Apple Super Pilot, an authoring language that can run on any Apple II computer with 64–128K of memory and two floppy disk drives, is quite simple for teachers to use and is easily integrated into other types of software applications.

With Super Pilot, all program statements are entered by means of the Lesson Text Editor. Text and questions that will appear in the computer lesson are also entered through the Editor. The user can test and "debug" the lesson (correct the errors in the program) through a testing procedure option within the Lesson Text Editor. A second editor, known as the Graphics Editor, allows the user to create visual aids to illustrate lesson concepts. Special sets of characters, such as large alphabet or mathematical symbols, can be designed and entered through another editor, the Character Set Editor. Another editor allows songs and other sound effects to be added.

Using an authoring language to create lessons does require a knowledge of CAI instructional design. The more experienced a teacher is with CAI instructional design, the more detailed and advanced the lesson to be developed. Time and discipline to learn to do it well are required of the teacher. Both authoring languages and authoring systems provide the means to create individually tailored instructional programs, but the limitations and requirements of each should be carefully considered and the value compared with commercially developed software packages.

The selection or development of appropriate software is a nontrivial task that requires training, attention to detail, and a knowledge of what instructional goals the software is to meet.

Hypermedia Concepts

HyperMedia, a major new direction in instruction, is (in the most basic form) a mechanism for creating nonlinear materials. Nonlinear materials are those in which the normal linear sequence of sentences, paragraphs, and the like is linked to alternate paths, allowing pictures, graphs, and so forth to be introduced into the body of the material. HyperMedia authoring programs used extensively include HyperCard (Apple), Linkway (IBM), Toolbook (A Symetrix), AmigaVision (Commodore), and Media-Text (Wings/Seaburst) (Venezby & Osin, 1991, 22–23, 246–252).

One illustrative package is HyperCard. This is a software package designed to be configured by the user. HyperCard allows a teacher to custom design a tutorial for which no commercially developed software is available. HyperCard also can be used for record keeping functions such as inventory, student records, and grade books.

The common metaphor for describing HyperCard is that of stacks of cards. Individual cards may be linked together in any combination or linked to other "stacks" of cards. Individual "cards" are linked together by the use of special "buttons" that are often disguised as "icons."

DEFINITION: Icon

A picture, symbol, or image that appears on a monitor that stands for its object and represents a command (e.g., file drawer to represent filing, trash can to represent trash).

Figure 5-1
A hypothetical stack
example.

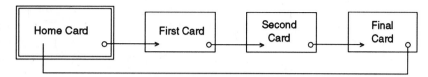

In all stacks, cards are seen one at a time on the screen and are connected by links called "buttons." The buttons are represented above by small circles.

Notice that the final card in the stack is connected to the "Home" card. This serves two purposes: it gives the user a place to go when finished with the stack, and it connects the user to the place of origin in HyperCard, the Home card.

Stack Design

Stacks can be designed in practically any configuration. When beginning a stack design it may be useful to compare two basic types of design configurations. For purposes of illustration the two types will be referred to as *linear* and *divergent* design.

In a linear design, the information is presented in sequential fashion, with little or no divergence from the information path. An advantage to this design is it is relatively easy to understand and link. Linear stack design offers fewer choices to the user and is less flexible than divergent designs; however, it may be the best choice for presenting some materials.

Divergent stack designs probably give the designer the most flexibility when authoring stacks. The author can make use of "menus" on one card that allow the student to make decisions about what path to follow, or perhaps to choose among several branches of the stack that offer different information.

Figure 5-3 illustrates the potential complexity of stack construction. It also underscores the importance of logical design before building, and the need to begin on a simple scale before attempting very large, complicated stacks.

There are no hard rules governing stack design. HyperCard was designed to be configured by the user. Whatever suits your purpose should determine the design you choose. A combination of linear and divergent styles would certainly be appropriate, if dictated by the content of the information.

Figure 5-2
Linear stack design
example.

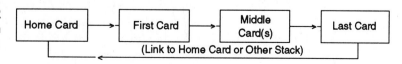

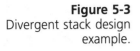

Figure 5-3
Divergent stack design
example.

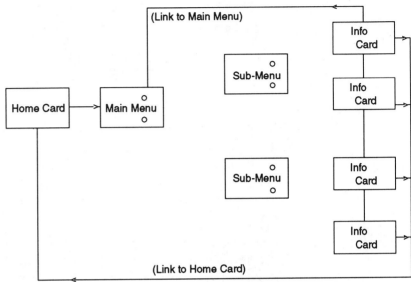

Evaluation

The evaluation of software is an important feature of any computer-based instructional plan or program. Much effort is needed to select appropriate, functional, cost-effective programs that meet instructional goals and objectives and
learners' needs in an appropriate way. When working with students with special
needs, an additional concern is the reading comprehension of selected subgroups
of students—especially those with a learning disability, mental retardation, or
hearing impairment. Many students with special needs have language deficiencies. When instructions appear on the screen—as is almost always the case with
CAI or CMI activities—the user (learner) must read, process, and follow these
directions. This can be a difficult task for many learners with special needs. Thus,
the additional evaluation need arises to review not only the content, graphics,
and objectives of a lesson, but also the readability of the instructional set. A final
concern is that some software packages have a built-in clock controlling access
time for sections and/or individual problems. For some programs, the author(s)
will set a time clock of so many seconds per problem to pace movement through
the program. Under normal circumstances, this time-oriented scheme is probably a useful tool. With certain students with special needs using a clock is yet
another hurdle to overcome. Teachers and other software evaluators should be
aware of such clock-oriented items and be prepared to make necessary additions
or alterations to the software to either disable the clock or increase time constraints to be more sensitive to learner needs.

It is difficult to judge whether educational software is appropriately user-friendly or efficient. This is difficult to determine for the casual user and even more difficult for learners with special needs. Teachers and support staff often do not have the time or expertise to evaluate software, so the major burden for software evaluation may be placed on either the building administrator, the school system computer coordinator, or the site-based software and hardware coordinator. Building administrators may have the skills in software evaluation, but no one would expect them to know all of the content materials as well as special needs required of the children with disabilities present in a classroom. As a result many users rely on outside experts to evaluate programs, based on established criteria. Some states even have a software evaluation group. Some local school systems band with universities, colleges, community colleges, technical institutes, and even businesses and industrial training sites to select the appropriate software. As site-based administrators have more and more responsibility for spending of funds, securing of hardware and software, and hiring of personnel, the selection of software based on both its effectiveness and efficiency becomes more and more of a problem. The ultimate decision should rest, of course, with the building administrator, the computer coordinator (if one is available), the individual members of the teaching faculty, and the students themselves if appropriate. The major concerns should include but are not limited to the following:

1. Can a copy of the material be obtained on approval, so the school system can try it before it is purchased? In general, if the software company will not allow materials to be tried it is a good rule not to deal with them.

2. What is the warranty on the software?

3. What is the vendor's responsibility for updating software when new editions are released, and how are these updates supplied to the system?

4. What additional costs will be involved for any updates, especially if these involve multiple copies of the same piece of software?

5. Are the directions for the secured software clearly written and understandable? Remember that reading, speed, and comprehension continue to be major concerns when dealing with children with disabilities.

6. What is the record-keeping or management system provided by the software?

7. Is the level of vocabulary and concepts appropriate for the students to be served?

8. Can the student or the teacher modify the software to change the amount of time the program allows for reading a passage and/or choosing an answer? This is especially important for students with disabling conditions where readability and reading time become major issues.

9. Are graphics and sound used, and if so are they appropriate for the disabling condition of the learner involved with the software package?

10. What are the type and extent of support services?

Even when outside experts' recommendations are used, the final decision should reside with the school administrator, subject area faculty, local building coordinator, and the students.

Identification Schema

IBM, Apple, and other major (and many minor) companies have provided substantial services to the educational community. Attention to the needs of special learners has also been a feature of the activities of many of these companies. One key feature in the support is represented in the schema for identification of software features useful for teachers as they select appropriate programs for use with students with special needs.

Children with special needs (physical, sensory, cognitive, emotional) are utilizing technology-based software and tools originally developed for non-disabled students. They need the support and skill of effective teachers who understand their learning characteristics. This requires that teachers be able to match the content and features of software to the needs and skills of their special education students.

In a 1991 publication, *IBM Educational Software: Integrating the Needs of Students in Special Education*, IBM provided a set of broad software features and then further categorized these into detailed elements (i.e., content, instructional strategies, etc.) that could be used by a teacher, parent, or administrator to examine an individual piece of software for possible use by students. The following material is excerpted from this extensive, and informative document.

Software Features

Instructional Methods

This category gives the teacher information on the type of instruction provided. Exclusive of content, level of instruction is probably the most important initial feature for selecting programs for use with special needs students. While most programs follow one primary method of instruction, some programs have more than one method of instruction.

—**drill and practice**

presents a problem and evaluates the student's response for correctness

—**tutorial**

provides instruction on a skill or concept

—**game**

provides a contest format for the introduction of material and/or for assessment of performance

—**problem solving**

problems are presented to solve based on skills or concepts introduced in or outside the program

—**simulation**

real-life scenarios to evaluate competencies in the target skills or concepts are presented

—**exploratory learning**

knowledge base(s) from which concepts are attained via teacher-guided or self-guided investigative browsing are presented

Content Level

In conjunction with instructional methods, the complexity of cognitive demands placed on a student are important for teachers to know when selecting software. This category is based on the five areas developed in Bloom's Taxonomy of Edu-

—**knowledge**

the student is expected to retain and recall some specific set of facts

—**comprehension**

the student is expected to understand the material in the lesson to the extent that the student can produce an explanation on demand

—**application**

the student applies the material presented to other situations through the use of general rules, rules of procedures, or generalized method

—**analysis**

the student uses the information learned in the lesson to solve problems which requires a break down of the information into concise, manageable components

—**synthesis**

the student incorporates the information from this lesson with other knowledge to synthesize new thought on related subjects cational Objectives: knowledge, comprehension, application, analysis, and synthesis.

Presentation Features

These features are important in matching the learning characteristics of the student to the courseware. Many educators teach to strengths and remediate weaknesses. Knowledge of presentation features allows the teacher to select instructional material that matches educational objectives with the individual learner's needs.

—visual prompts
student is guided and prompted through visual cues

—high-quality graphics
uses (or has an option for using) higher-resolution graphics monitors to display clearer, more realistic images

—auditory prompts
student is guided and prompted through auditory cues

—key words highlighted
highlighting indicates desired responses, "what to do next," or other information important to the student

—animation

uses animated graphics

—consistent presentation format

menus, functional keys, and presentation formats remain consistent throughout the lesson

—voice
uses speech that requires an internal or external adaptation

—print options
printout of the user's screen is available during the lesson using a print function

—graphics
uses nontext graphics (e.g., pictures and drawings)

Input Features

This category allows the teacher to know whether the software uses consistent input from the student. Ability to make corrections may also be important depending on the objectives of the teacher and the needs of the individual students. Keystroke requirements are also important for some students in special education.

> —**consistency of requested input**
>
> type of required input needed to proceed through the program is consistent (e.g., spacebar to advance; function keys have only one meaning each throughout the program)
>
> —**minimal keystroke input**
>
> type of input required is limited to one or two keystrokes (e.g., spacebar to advance; a single letter in response to a multiple-choice question)
>
> —**opportunity to correct input**
>
> allows the user to change answers by use of a backspace or an erase key

Feedback to User Response

The features under this category provide the basis for consistent intervention with children. Errorless learning is enhanced by features that provide assistance to the student either on request or as a result of errors.

> —**help/hints available**
>
> on-demand or error-driven help is available
>
> —**wrong answer assistance**
>
> wrong answers are followed by a review of the material, help screens, an opportunity to reenter a correct answer
>
> —**variety of reinforcers**
>
> student is offered a variety of reinforcers for correct responses
>
> —**consistent feedback**
>
> same types of feedback are given for various responses (e.g., program always returns user to a main menu when lessons are completed; if voice is used for positive reinforcement, it is used each time a correct response is given)

Presentation Options

These options include information on whether the teacher can control and modify the type, content, and level of instruction delivered to the student. It also provides information on whether the student and teacher can track daily individual progress within the courseware.

—**user-controlled movement**

user is able to select a starting point in a lesson, move to other points within a lesson without exiting, and exit a lesson from any point

—**bookmark feature**

a feature that marks where the student exited the program and then allows for reentry to that location

—**control presentation pace**

teacher can slow down or speed up the pace of presentation or define time periods between evaluations

—**control difficulty level**

program has distinct difficulty levels and the teacher can control the entry point for students with respect to level of difficulty

—**modify/select lesson content**

teacher can make selections or generate material to be included in the lesson (e.g., incorporate individual word lists into a drill and practice program)

—**modify response to wrong answers**

teacher can select responses to incorrect answers, and/or can modify the type of response to incorrect answers (help screens, review content, etc.)

—**sound on/off**

user or teacher has the option of turning the sound on or off

Assessment Activity Features

These features provide information regarding control of evaluation, type of reporting, and analysis of student performance that is available to the teacher. This information is useful for maintaining data, developing and monitoring IEP information, and sharing information with students and parents.

—**modify/select evaluation context**

teacher can modify or select the items to be included in the evaluation

—**issues descriptive reports**

program reports on student performance in terms of keystrokes, number correct, chapters completed, and the like

—**issues analytical reports**

program reports on percentages, variance in individual's performance across lessons, variance across a class of students taking the same lessons, and/or individual student performances against normative data

Support Materials

These features highlight what additional materials are available to the teacher. These materials enhance the ability of the teacher to integrate the courseware into the general curriculum as well as identify appropriate instructional goals and objectives for students with special needs.

—instruction manual

explains procedures for installing and running the program

—curriculum integration guide

provides suggestions for incorporation of lesson material into the classroom curriculum

—learning objectives

provides a list of well-defined learning objectives to complement standard curriculum or to include in an IEP

—instructional materials

provides additional worksheets or materials that may aid in the learning of the lesson

---

Learning to Select and Use Software

The decision to purchase a software package is a major one for a school or school system. However, the purchase decision must then be translated into use by the practitioner. Clearly the need for training by the end-user is a factor to be considered. Proper early training has two important features. First, without proper training, most software packages are simply not used or not used in an effective, efficient manner. Second, proper training in the use of each package maximizes its utility. General estimations show that from one-third to one-half the time is needed to have a package taught by a trainer compared with self-teaching. Even though a teacher for a package is a cost consideration, the overall usefulness of the package and the correct utilization of the work make this money well spent.

Materials supplied with software packages are necessary, and selection of the package can be greatly influenced by the quality of manuals and other documentation. The inclusion of the help menu, error lists, and possibly a toll-free telephone number are features of many complex, multipurpose software packages.

Classes for users of software are important, but it may also be important to see that users of the output of the program are involved in the educational program. For students with special needs, parents and professional staff may need to be involved in the interpretation of the output of selected software packages.

For example, the results of a software package producing an IEP or some other plan may need extensive explanation of how to use the printed results. In some instances confidentiality of the results is also an issue.

While there is a real tendency to try to deal with concrete, specific information in applications software, keying on a limited number of applications is counterproductive. Teachers and students are the best judges of the use of a piece of software and its applicability.

One of the strengths of teacher judgment—and one of the real challenges—is the ability to use a single software package in multiple situations. The idea that a *specific* piece of software is used to solve a *specific* problem can be counterproductive to how applications software should be used. The ability of the teacher to use software to assist a wide variety of students with a wide variety of disabilities is one of the key concerns in the effective and efficient use of software. To use the same applications package for a student with a hearing impairment and for a student who has a learning disability is what teachers do—and do well. (Appendix G shows a software evaluation form for teachers. It will be helpful in determining where to start.) One of many references for software evaluation is published by the Northeast Regional Exchange and the Southwest Educational Development Laboratory (*Evaluation of Educational Software*, 1983).

Improving Software

When CAI emerged in the late 1950s and early 1960s, much of the cognitive theory and research now available was not in place. Programs that helped students learn how to learn, how to set cognitive goals, and how to apply effective strategies were not yet written.

Authors like Gerald Bracey (1988), Director of Research and Evaluation for Englewood, Colorado Schools, provide a list of items that software developers should note. These include:

- Make knowledge construction activities overt
- Maintain attention to cognitive goals
- Treat a student's lack of knowledge in a positive way
- Provide process-relevant feedback
- Encourage learning strategies other than rehearsal
- Encourage multiple passes through information
- Support varied ways for students to organize their knowledge
- Encourage maximum use and examination of existing knowledge
- Provide opportunities for reflection and take into account individual learning style

- Facilitate transfer of knowledge across contexts
- Give students more responsibility for contributing to one another's learning

Statistical Software

As teachers and systems become more at ease with the computer and its many applications, the use of software packages to analyze statistical data becomes more of a possibility. The idea that regular classroom teachers will become research professionals and analyze large quantities of data may not be practical. However, teachers, resource personnel, and administrators often do have problems that require or raise the issue of statistical comparisons between groups of scores or as the results of certain instructional applications. These can be handled through the use of microcomputer and statistical packages such as PCSTAT or Statistical Analysis System (SAS) for the PC. Many statistical packages require the availability of substantially more memory than is required for normal use, but the need for this additional memory (core) can generally be confined to one machine that services the entire classroom or even the entire building. These machines also can often be used to build transmittable files for local, state, and even federal reports.

Administrative Support

The constraints of the administrators' and teachers' imagination are the only limits to the administrative application of the computer for pupils. Many of these applications are related to all pupils, but the administrative issues of bus routing for pupils with special needs has a specific application. The maintainence of extensive records and their accessibility are other potential considerations. Administrative work relative to final reports is always an issue, but perhaps more so when funding and reporting requirements for students with special needs are the areas of interest.

Numerous packages are available; the selection is wide and the costs are variable. Skill in identification of what is needed is the key to appropriate selection of software packages.

Data Security

Security of data files is a concern for anyone associated with computer database systems or individual data files. This concern may even be more critical when dealing with data on individual students. These data would include test scores, IEP information, medical and psychological test results, and various elements of background data. Availability of most student data is on a "need to know" basis with the control procedures known to the persons using the files and available to persons requesting information. Most school systems routinely close files and the access to these items is restricted.

Much of the security system surrounding student data is a people system, but computer security items are crucial. The ability to access data files from terminals and in some instances from touch type telephones makes the security issue one of concern for the computer system manager. The traditional security system of passwords and other entry controls works well and is a feature of any effective, efficient system. Care should be taken in clearance of the personnel associated with data entry and data report production.

Security also extends to the ability of a system to produce reports that contain the appropriate information on a regular basis. The need to back up files and to provide electrical and mechanical protection is a given with any data processing system. Most experts agree that system files should be backed up at least once a day and perhaps as often as twice a day during peak data entry times. This backup should be on a disk file and stored at a location away from the entry site. Most data storage facilities provide fireproof and theft-proof facilities for such items. The need to provide a hard copy backup for data files is at the discretion of the teachers and site administrators.

Clearly, security is a concern for all persons associated with data entry and file maintenance. The need to secure information and to provide it to authorized users on a need-to-know basis is the key to an effectively utilized system.

Accuracy and completeness are other issues for the teacher and the data entry personnel to address. Their attention to detail and to the correctness of what is entered have direct bearing on the success of the day-to-day work of the teachers.

File Backups

File backups for personal computer software is normally acquired from a vendor, public domain clearinghouse, or an associate. With use, the personal computer acquires data files. These data may enter the computer through the keyboard, from disks, through scanning, or even over a phone line via modem. The user may create data that is processed from other data. An example of this might be the extraction of demographic data on a student from a personal history data file and grade reporting data from an end of the semester data file to produce a new file including both personal and grade information.

The user is well advised to back up data files regularly. A computer hard disk might fail, a "floppy" disk might be demagnetized, or the electrical power might fail when the disk is being written on. Any of these problems might cause the computer and user to lose valuable data and/or programs. This loss might not be recoverable. For example, if a vendor list written to a hard disk is lost, then the material might need to be researched, recompiled, and reentered. At the least, reentry is tedious, lengthy, and error-prone. At the worst, the research needs to be replicated if the records (raw data) are still available.

DEFINITION: Floppy Disk

A flexible disk (*diskette*) of oxide-coated mylar that is stored in paper or plastic envelopes. The entire envelope is inserted into the disk unit. Floppy disks provide low-cost storage that is used widely with minicomputers and microcomputers. Floppy disks were originally developed for low-capacity storage, low costs, and relatively low data transfer rates. Regular floppy disks have a diameter of 20.32 cm (8 inches), mini floppy disks have a diameter of 13.3 cm (5¼ inches), and micro floppy disks have a diameter of 7.6 cm (3 inches).

Another disk has been developed for use with selected microcomputers. It is enclosed in a "hard" container, is 3½ inches in diameter, and can store three (3) times as much information as the 5¼ inch diskette.

The wise user will back up programs and data on a routine basis. These backups are typically done by a software utility that writes the information from the disk to a backup medium such as a small cartridge tape or floppy diskette. Many personal computers in active environments are backed up on a weekly basis. However, the activity is not simple. A 20 megabyte hard disk could take up to 50 floppy diskettes or one cartridge tape (similar to a VCR tape) to do a complete hard disk file backup.

Legal Issues

Legal issues and concerns must be considered in the day-to-day operation of each special needs classroom (and all other classrooms). Perhaps the concerns about the legal issues, especially the invasion of privacy, are more a part of the regular concerns of special needs teachers than others in public and private schools. Issues of availability and protection of applied records, test scores, and psychological profiles as well as IEPs have long been concerns of teachers of children with special needs. The computer's strengths—the ability to process, store, and make available large amounts of data—can lead to possible abuses of the distribution of such items. Unprotected data files or careless distribution of printed materials can create situations where confidential information is released to unauthorized users. Generally, all files should be protected in some way. For example, in WordPerfect, a widely used word-processing package, a file(s) may be "password" protected. This means that upon entering the system, a potential user is asked to provide a symbol, word, or phrase that "clears" the user to have access to such information. The term *code* often is used. This is used to protect both data files, and programs that may also be stored in the computer. Release of data on an as-needed basis is a good practice, but each teacher, site manager, and school district must develop a policy covering the distribution of data. The policy should be written and distributed to appropriate persons as well as available for distribution upon request. The policy must be explained to persons having responsibility for entry and use of data files and reports.

Piracy

Many teachers and other school faculty and/or staff as well as students often are tempted to copy a computer program offered by a friend or colleague. A seemingly harmless activity, this is really piracy and care must be taken to avoid such things as unauthorized copying of programs. Additionally, teachers need to be cognizant of the issues of site licensure associated with the use of labs having network capability. Generally the ownership of a copy of a program, complete with documentation, does *not* mean the same program can be loaded onto a host machine and then become available to any or all units on the network. Most networks operate using a file server—a high-capacity disk storage device (or computer)—which each computer on the network accesses for retrieving a file or program. These files or programs can then, as noted above, be shared by all computers with access to the network (since a program—once loaded—can be retrieved by an attached machine). Thus the seemly harmless loading of a program to make it accessible to multiple users usually violates most copyrights, unless a site license is obtained.

Software License

Copyrights and compliance with the law are major concerns for schools and school districts. The following sections cover the law, upgrades, and local area networks. (Appendix H contains a copy of *EDUCOM*'s 1987 Statement on Software Copyrights.)

The Law. According to Title 17 of the U.S. Code, the copyright owner is given certain exclusive rights, including the right to make and distribute copies (Section 106). The law further states that "anyone who violates any of the exclusive rights of the copyright owner . . . is an infringer of the copyright" (Section 501). The only exception is the user's right to make a backup copy for archival purposes (Section 117).

In general, the copyright law means that for each user there should be one legitimate, purchased copy. The copyright law makes no distinction between duplicating software for sale or duplicating it for free distribution. The law protects the exclusive rights of the copyright owner. It does not give users the right to copy software unless the manufacturer does not provide a backup copy.

Unauthorized duplication of software is a federal crime. Penalties may include fines up to $100,000 and jail terms up to five years. Although software is a new medium of intellectual property, its protection is grounded in the long-established rules that govern other more familiar media, such as records, books, and films.

Upgrades. Software upgrades are considered improvements to the original software, not new copies. If you have purchased an upgrade, do not continue to use the older version. Do not pass it on to another user.

LANs. License agreements for most software packages include restrictions for use on a LAN. It is a violation of most license agreements to place a single-copy version on a LAN for simultaneous access by more than one user. Many publishers offer multiuser versions of their software designed specifically for use on a LAN.

Summary

There is little question that hardware (and assistive devices in the main) are generally useless without something to "drive" them. That something is software —the programs that cause computers to do what computers do. These "commands" or "direction sets" make the hardware perform calculations, respond to a light sensor, provide a printed page, or illuminate screens.

The responsibility for producing such sets of instructions or "programs" falls to a programmer, who may tell systems what to do or tell students what to do. Programs are short or long, simple or complex, external device dependent or independent. Programs instruct directly, provide a method or format to provide instruction, or are part of the operating system of the computer. They are but a set of commands produced by programmers to "instruct" the computer to accomplish tasks from simple to complex. These tasks are the basis for construction of software packages and systems for use with all types of computers.

References

Bracey, G. W. (1988). Computers and anxiety in education. *Electronic Learning, 8* (3), 26–28.

Behrmann, M. M., Mittler, J., Taber, F., & Rumbarger, A. R. (1991). *IBM educational software: Integrating the needs of students in special education.* IBM.

Evaluation of Educational Software. (1983). Austin, TX: The Northeast Regional Exchange & Southwest Educational Development Laboratory.

MacArthur, C. A., & Malouf, D. B. (1991). Teachers' beliefs, plans, and decisions about computer-based instruction. *Journal of Special Education, 25* (1), 44–71.

Schank, R. C. (1987–1988). Creativity education: A standard for computer based teaching. *Machine Mediated Learning, 2* (3), 175–194.

Venezky, R., & Osin, L. (1991). *The intelligent design of computer-assisted instruction* (pp. 22–23, 246–252). White Plains, NY: Longman Publishing Group.

Assistive Devices: Vision

Objectives

After reading this chapter, you should be able to:

- Discuss integration of assistive devices into an instructional program.
- Discuss how to determine usefulness of assistive devices.
- Determine multiple uses for an assistive device.
- Distinguish between students with vision problems and those with decoding problems.
- Describe input and output assistive devices for persons with vision impairment or with decoding problems.

This chapter deals with those assistive devices designed to facilitate the learning of students with vision disabilities. As has been established in Chapter 1 of this text, the facilitation of learning for students with special needs is not without difficulty. The degree of difficulty is, of course, related to the severity and nature of the disabling condition, the availability of special equipment, and the expertise of the individual instructor(s) working with the learner. In general, the learner's adaptability to assistive devices, whether computer-controlled or not, is directly related to the effectiveness of the instructor in providing the motivation to utilize any particular device.

The number of devices available for student use presents a mind-boggling list. Appendix I contains a partial listing (which would really need to be updated on an almost daily basis) of assistive device materials and equipment. Assistive devices that are not an integral part of the instructional program or of independent living skills are of little assistance to a student with a disability. Figure 6-1 illustrates the frequency with which assistive devices are used by persons with disabilities. The use of the device needs to be built into the instructional program, and the results of the instructional or independent living skills program need to be dependent on (at least in part) the use of the assistive device utilized. In some instances the choice among assistive devices must be based on the number of pupils who will profit from the use of the device, the availability of the device, the availability of support for the device in terms of technical support and repair or maintenance services, and, finally, the bottom line of economic consideration.

Perhaps overly simplistic, but nevertheless useful, the following six questions can be used in determining which assistive devices are useful for particular applications (Green & Brightman, 1990):

1. Above all, does the product help the student access a computer?
2. Is it satisfying to use?
3. Is it difficult to learn to use?
4. What does it cost?
5. What computer systems does the product work on?
6. Does it work with all software programs, or only specialized ones?

Many assistive devices stand alone (i.e., all the devices either replace or augment an existing piece of equipment). For example, TDD augments the telephone. A TDD allows a person who is deaf to use a standard telephone. Other devices make a piece of equipment operate in a different manner (e.g., slower). A large number of assistive devices, however, require that a piece of software be utilized with them for successful operation. The reader should note this singular or dual requirement, which is a feature of many special needs applications.

Figure 6-1
Frequency of assistive
devices. Source: Center
for Special Education
Technology, September,
1988 *The Marketplace,*
Vol. 1, No. 2.

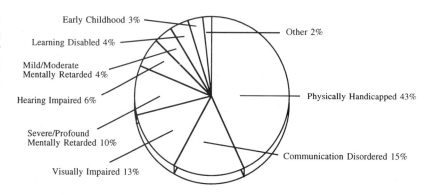

The severity level of the disability and the disability type have a major impact on the delivery of services. Again, this text supports the basic position of mainstreaming and, even more important, the multiple use of computers, assistive devices, and software to facilitate the most effective and efficient use of those resources available to the classroom teacher and the student.

Some devices may be used to "assist" in more than one disability. (See Figure 6-3 for some examples of the multiple uses of assistive devices.) The set of devices available for persons who are characterized as having a vision impairment represents by far the largest group. The quality and "real" usefulness of these devices can only be determined in practice and observation of the use for which each is intended.

Readers should be cautioned that products and the companies selling and servicing them come and go all the time. Information available today (including

Figure 6-2
TDD: Telecommunication
Device for the Deaf.
*Courtesy of International
Business Machines
Corporation.*

Figure 6-3
Some examples of
assistive devices'
multiple uses.

Assistive Device	Learner Characteristic
Text-to-Voice	—trouble with reading —vision problem —beginning reader who needs help
Telecommunications Device for the Deaf (TDD)	—hearing loss precludes telephone use —needs practice writing one's thoughts clearly (may or may not have hearing loss) —needs practice reading at a faster rate (TDD requires that one must be able to read at the speed the other person types)
Word Predictor Program	—restricted mobility necessitates this kind of help to increase speed of composition —has trouble spelling, but can identify the desired word when it is listed —needs practice with differentiating words that begin with same or similar spelling
Word Processing	—needs practice editing or rewriting compositions —loves to compose stories, but becomes frustrated trying to polish hand-written work —needs help organizing written work —needs practice outlining correctly (most software programs contain an OUTLINE function)

pricing) may or may not be accurate next week. "Comparison shopping" still makes sense.

Organization of the Sections on Assistive Devices

While all persons with disabilities have varied functional requirements, the basic breakdown of devices falls into the categories of input assistance and output assistance. While the severity of the disability or the combination of disabilities must be taken into account, the sections that follow deal with one disability grouping at a time taken from the list below. The vision section is extensive. Many assistive devices designed for persons with vision impairments are useful for persons whose eyes work but who may have processing problems. For example, some students with learning disabilities can "see" but can't make sense of what they see. Since this text emphasizes learner characteristics rather than disability label, the organization of this assistive devices section reflects that emphasis.

Common Grouping of Assistive Devices for Use with Varied Disability Categories

1. **Vision**
2. **Hearing**
3. **Learning**
4. **Speech and Language**
5. **Mobility**

Vision*

This section addresses students who cannot *recognize* (decode) letters and those who have substantial difficulty with *seeing* (clarity or comprehensiveness). The first category includes students who have a learning disability that involves the inability to differentiate certain letters. Some students who have had strokes or other types of brain damage may have similar difficulty. The second category includes students who have a vision impairment (blindness, partial vision, low vision). Both types of students may have similar difficulties in the classroom or with materials and be able to use the same pieces of computer access equipment.

Students with Decoding Problems

Students who have experienced head injuries may sometimes lose the ability to distinguish one letter from another or to "see" the entire picture. Depending on the location of the damage to the brain, a student may see a *b*, but name it a *d*; or the student may see the *b* as a *q*. A student who has been diagnosed as having a specific learning disability may have a similar problem. In either case, a page of printed characters may be indecipherable as letters or words and bear no resem-

---

*The material for the vision section was written by Norma Tedder, Ph.D., and Rose Angelocci of the University of New Orleans.

blance to audible language. Teachers who specialize in this type of learning disability may be able to provide compensatory techniques that will allow the student to read, but the student may still find reading print a laborious process. Such students may benefit from an auditory alternative. For others, materials in print cannot be made meaningful. The only possible input mode for these students may be auditory. These students may be assessed and served by teachers who specialize in serving students with learning disabilities or teachers who specialize in serving children with medically fragile conditions or neurological or orthopedic problems. They may be served by other "specialists" as well. These children may have additional disabilities, but will be included in a regular classroom for at least part of the day.

Students Who Cannot See Well

Blindness is a legal term that relates to the clarity (acuity) or comprehensiveness (visual field) of an individual's ability to see. A person whose acuity (in the better eye with best correction) is limited to seeing at 20 feet what a "normal" person sees at 200 feet is said to be legally blind. Normal vision is called "20/20"; legal blindness is abbreviated as "20/200". That vision is for recognizing objects at a distance. Also included in the legal blindness category is a person who sees only 20 degrees of the normal 180 degrees of the peripheral field. That remaining 20 degrees of vision may be in any area: straight ahead, up, down, or to the side. There may be several of these vision windows, but the largest, in the better eye, will be only 20 degrees for the individual who is legally blind.

Although the student who is legally blind will almost always have difficulty with printed classroom materials, there are other students with functional limitations in either their acuity or field of vision that will influence their educational program. Students who have visual windows of larger than 20 degrees, students whose visual acuity of 20/70 to 20/200, and students who are progressively losing their vision are not legally blind, but usually have a functional vision limitation that poses a handicap to their educational progress. Figure 6-4 illustrates what a boon assistance devices can be.

Braille

Braille is a tactile way of reading and writing for many people who are blind, but not every student will need or use braille. A braille cell consists of 6 dots in a 2 × 3 matrix. There are 63 combinations of dots that can represent symbols, which may differ according to context. Braille users refer to "grade" levels of braille. Grade I refers to the alphabet, numbers, and punctuation symbols. Grade II is the level used for most reading materials. It incorporates shorthand codes that use one or more symbols to represent groups of letters or whole words. For example, the symbol for the letter *c* (Grade I) becomes the word *can* in Grade II. Reading

Figure 6-4
The PC is My Lifeline.
*Source: PC
Computing,* Vol. 2,
#7, July 1989, p. 87.

Imagine yourself blindfolded with your ears plugged. No light, no sound. That's what it means to be deaf and blind. How would you be able to use a PC? Read the manuals that come with DBASE IV? Communicate with others? Hold a full-time job as a computer professional?

It's all possible.

I was born deaf and sighted and gradually lost my vision. Adaptive devices did not exist when I enrolled as a student at New York University, so I depended on my usable sight to complete the required reading; I received my bachelor's degree summa cum laude with a major in mathematics. When I was doing graduate work in statistics at NYU, I began using a VTEK magnification system, which I continued to use in my work as a computer programmer. The system enlarges printed material and displays it on a TV-like monitor.

Since then, my vision has deteriorated, and I use other devices in my work and in my life. I have worked for several high-tech companies and am currently a senior programmer/

analyst at Wang Laboratories in Lowell, Massachusetts. I work as a tele-commuter from home and make weekly trips to the office. Though I still rely on fingerspelling for face-to-face conversations, I use a variety of devices in my work.

Optacon gives me immediate and independent access to printed material—computer manuals, books, and even simple graphic images on a bed of vibrating pins that I feel with my index finger, one character at a time.

With VersaBraille II Plus, I can operate the AT-compatible Wang PC280 that I use at home. A portable braille terminal that can stand alone or connect to a PC or mainframe, it provides a 20-character braille display, or window, of what is on the screen. Special software enables me to navigate a 25-line-by-80-character PC screen.

These devices allow me to use off-the-shelf MS-DOS software such as WordPerfect, Lotus 1-2-3, DBASE III Plus and DBASE IV, ProComm, and PC programming language compilers.

I write software

and documentation on the PC in languages such as COBOL, C, and DBASE III Plus using a regular text editor (KEdit from Mansfield Software Group). I compile, test, and debug the programs on the PC. When I'm working on mainframe programs, I use a high-speed modem and a terminal emulator to turn the PC into a workstation that runs off the Wang mainframe in Lowell, several miles away. In this mode, my VersaBraille helps me navigate the mainframe menus and get access to the company's electronic mail system, Wang Office. Through electronic mail, I also discuss technical issues and exchange information with my colleagues.

But the PC is more than a professional device for me. With the PC, I can hold telephone communications with anyone else who has a PC and modem, I have met many people through nationwide computer services like Delphi and CompuServe. On Delphi, I participate in computer conferences several times a week, chat with

(continued)

Figure 6-4
(*Continued*)

other computer enthusiasts around the country, and use electronic mail to keep in touch with them at other times. I also get news and weather reports online and occasionally play games; my favorite is a word game called Scrambel. Because my disabilities are not visible to other users online, they have been surprised, on the rare occasions when I mention it, to find out that I am deaf and blind.

Adaptive device technology is at a point now where it can help disabled people like myself to live constructive and productive lives.

However, these sophisticated devices must keep up with changes in PC technology. Most devices work only on MS-DOS-based systems and do not address operating systems such as Unix and OS/2. Not all special software can tell the user where highlighted words appear on the screen; the PC community must consider putting graphics into a format accessible to those who can't see the screen. And the equipment must be made affordable.

But with all that remains to be done, the technology is helping people. Without the PC and adaptive devices, my life would be much more lonely and solitary. I could not read all the books I want to read, and I probably wouldn't be working in a field that interests me. I would have far fewer opportunities to communicate and joke with others. Optacon, Versa-Braille, and the PC have enhanced my life professionally, socially, and intellectually. —Barbara Wagreich

_____

Barbara Wagreich is a senior programmer and analyst at Wang Laboratories.

braille is a slow process. The average braille reader can read between 90 and 120 words per minute, in contrast to the average print reading rate of 250 to 300 words per minute for a high school student.

A medical (ophthalmological) eye examination is usually required to refer a student for the services of a "vision teacher" (an education specialist who works with students with vision problems). However, the vision teacher is the person who performs a functional vision assessment to determine the student's need for adapted educational services. The educational vision specialist will make recommendations regarding print size, contrast, type face, optimal lighting for various tasks, placement of materials, and alternatives to regular print (such as braille), if needed. Some students with vision problems may not require a special reading medium. For example, a student may have 10 degrees of remaining visual field right in the center of his or her vision and be able to read regular print with no problem. This student might require other types of "vision" accommodations that are not related to computer use and print reading. The student with a vision problem may also have other disabilities and require additional specialists and modifications in the learning environment. Most students with vision disabilities

Figure 6-5
Alternative key pad.
*Courtesy of International
Business Machines
Corporation.*

will be seen in regular classrooms with adapted materials and equipment, including computers and special computer access devices.

Computer Access Devices and Related Equipment

Students who need an alternative to regular print and will be using a computer may require another way to enter information (input modifications). Other students may require an alternative to reading print from the screen or an alternative to ordinary print output. These devices are termed *output modifications.* There are several varieties and combinations.

Some students may require both input and output modifications of several types. A student may wish to input in braille and also output in braille in order to do her own proofreading; she may wish to convert to print output for the final draft of a writing assignment to give to her teacher. She would require both an input and output modification.

Input Devices

Many students with vision problems will actually have an advantage with computer input because most of them have been taught to type in the first or second grade. Therefore, most students discussed in this chapter may be able to use the regular computer keyboard (QWERTY), but there are alternative input

Figure 6-6
Vision: Use of alternative key pad showing highlighted screen. *Courtesy of International Business Machines Corporation.*

devices for those who cannot. These include devices that allow direct input from a brailler and those that translate keystrokes from an adapted keyboard into braille. These devices will work with other adaptations to produce the desired type of output. Teachers may also need to review the equipment used for students with mobility problems as well as the equipment described in this chapter.

Braille-to-Print Devices. The standard keyboard may be adapted so that just six keys of the regular keyboard can be used to input braille. There are software packages that allow this adaptation: BRLkeys for the IBM (may be used with any word-processing application); Gateway and VIEW2 (any application) which accompany Navigator; and special, self-contained word-processing programs, such as MegaDots (for IBM compatible) and BRAILLE-EDIT Xpress (BEX) for the Apple II. Using the regular computer keyboard has the advantage of providing full access to the function keys, which are important in many software applications such as WordPerfect, LOTUS 123, and dBaseIII+.

Braille-to-"Other" Devices. Some devices convert braille input to print, braille, both modes, or even voice output. Some devices, such as MPrint, do not attach directly to the computer. Instead, they use an electronic card to interface a manual Perkins brailler with a computer printer to produce printed output from braille input. The brailler will simultaneously produce a braille copy for the student.

DEFINITION: Refreshable Braille Display

Also known as a dynamic display, this system uses a set of braille cells, each consisting of six to eight retractable electronically operated reeds. An electronic code sent to the system raises and lowers the reeds to form braille characters that the individual can feel by placing his or her fingers on the top of the display. The first cell recomposes itself and fills up when the display is full.

Braille versions of portable note-taking devices are also available. The Braille 'n Speak (Blazie Engineering) combines a portable note-taking device, Perkins brailler style keypad, and voice output. The BrailleMate (TeleSensory) combines a portable note-taking device with braille keypad, voice output, and a single refreshable braille cell output. All of these devices have the capability of sorting information within the device itself or transferring the information to external disk drives, braille and print devices, or other computers.

Morse Code Input Systems. Another method for entering information into the computer is to use a dual-switch device to enter Morse code or Morse alphabet. Morse code consists of a system of short and long signals, universally known as "dits" and "dahs" (the code equivalent of the letter *P*, for example, is "dit dah dit"). Long and short signals can be sent to the computer by activating the

Figure 6-7
Power-Pad: An alternative input device. *Courtesy of International Business Machines Corporation.*

appropriate switch. Sometimes the computer will signal with different tones to confirm that a dit or a dah was entered. Ke:nx is a software compatible for use with Morse Code.

Output Devices

There may be one or more output choices that will make computer use possible for a student with print reading difficulties. There are three choices for output:

1. Synthetic speech and other "talking" devices

2. Image enhancement devices (large-print)

3. Braille and other tactual equipment

Synthetic Speech and Other Talking Devices. Synthetic speech or "talking" devices are not new or particularly unique. Many people have watches that talk, or even sing, to them. Alarm clocks are programmed to deliver "spoken" messages. Calculators and children's toys have "spoken" for years. Many health aids (scales, thermometers, blood pressure monitors, and blood glucose monitors) as well as answering machines and videocassette recorders (VCRs) are equipped with voice synthesis. There is even a "talking wallet" that voices the denomination of paper money.

Synthetic speech or "talking computers" allow the computer user to "hear" what is displayed on the screen. This is accomplished through a combination of hardware (voice synthesizer) and software (screen reading program) components. The hardware required may include a special computer board that must be installed in the computer and an external speaker that plugs into the computer board. Software programs will allow the user to change voice characteristics and to prompt the reading of specific portions of the screen.

There are several considerations in assembling a speech package. Voice synthesizers and screen reading programs must be compatible with each other and with the intended computer. IBM and IBM-compatible equipment cannot use synthesizers or screen reading program combinations designed for the Apple II computer family.

Another consideration is voice quality and response time. Synthesizers with higher speech quality are often more easily understood by the student with less training time required. However, they have slower response times and are more expensive. The clarity of these synthesizers may be particularly suitable for students with learning disabilities or hearing difficulties. DigiVox can record a quantity of spoken messages for all occasions, and play them back with a simple touch whenever they're needed (see Figure 6-8). Other synthesizers (such as Artic Transport by Artic Technologies) may be entirely appropriate for situations addressing routine data entry, which requires optimal response time and may be

Figure 6-8
DigiVox. *Courtesy of Sentient Systems Technology Inc.*

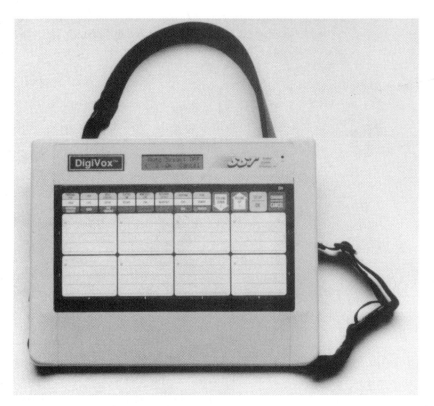

acceptable for reading uses. The specific needs of the learner should be part of the purchase equation.

Screen reading software should allow a user to change voice characteristics such as pitch, rate, tone, and volume; and they should work with a variety of voice synthesizers and applications. Screen reading software should be interactive with the application (WordPerfect, etc.) and should also allow for a "review" feature that lets the user roam freely about the screen without fear of making changes to previously entered text. Users should quickly and easily be able to read characters, words, or lines, as well as screen messages (such as "block," "margins," or other status messages). Control over spoken punctuation and the recognition of screen attributes (such as color) are also important. Users should be able to customize the software according to the application. Popular screen reading software for the IBM includes Vocal-Eyes (GW Micro), Artic Vision or Business Vision (Artic Technologies), Vert Plus (Telesensory, Inc.), and JAWS (Henter-Joyce, Inc.). The Apple II family uses the Texttalker for screen access. The Macintosh systems use a program called OutSPOKEN (Berkeley Systems) or

Write:OutLoud (Don Johnson Developmental Equipment, Inc.). Sound-Proof (Humanware, Inc.) is synthetic speech software that combines high-quality speech with screen enhancement features that highlight portions of the screen for users who are not totally blind.

Write:OutLoud is a program for the Macintosh that is an easy-to-use word processor with specialized speech "talk-back" features and easy access to common commands.

The speech options of Write:OutLoud let the user hear letters, words, or sentences as they are typed. Words can be highlighted while they are spoken. Users can also repeat the document in a number of ways: the whole document may be spoken, sentences can be spoken, or selected words and phrases can be spoken. The user can save the document and use it later for storytelling, reinforcement, multisensory learning, or communication.

While the word processing is uncomplicated, Write:OutLoud has important features such as a talking spell checker and "find" feature and a spelling monitor that cues the user if an unfamiliar word is typed. It has a "print one" feature that sends the document directly to the printer, eliminating a step by not displaying the print dialog box. It is suitable for both children and adult computer users. It has many size, font, style, and color choices.

There are currently no programs that convert graphics into another medium. Companies are progressively using more icons, windows, and other visual control technology. It is a challenge to the industry to produce software that will make graphics accessible to people with vision impairments.

Synthesized speech packages can be used in desktop computers or in portable computers. Voice synthesizers can be installed in IBM and IBM-compatible laptop computers so that students may use such technology in any setting. Portable synthesizers, such as the Artic Transport, do not require internal computer boards, but plug into the serial port of an IBM-compatible computer and allow the user to move the synthesizer from one computer to another. The portable synthesizers can be used in notebook computers for which no internal synthesizer is yet available. Speech output may be seen in such portable note-taking devices as the Braille n' Speak (Blazie Engineering) and the BrailleMate (TeleSensory).

LapTalker is a portable IBM-compatible computer with a built-in speech synthesizer. The rate of speech may be regulated from 70 to 450 words per minute. Two audio jacks, one for an external speaker and one for headphones, and a built-in internal speaker are included. Most screen reading programs can be used with this system.

Image Enhancement. Image enhancement may include print enlargement, screen enhancement, or both (Figure 6-9). Some students may benefit from the enhancement features contained in the applications already in use in the

Figure 6-9
Enlarged print as it
appears on a computer
monitor. *Courtesy of
International Business
Machines Corporation.*

classroom with the addition of a color monitor. Enhancement of the computer
screen can be as simple as changing the colors on the screen. Many everyday
computer applications allow the user to set background and foreground colors
(e.g., yellow letters on a blue background) to maximize a user's reading effectiveness. Traditional solutions to large print have included the use of oversized
monitors in place of regular computer screens, closed circuit televisions
(CCTVs), and hardware devices that display the information of the computer
screen on a separate monitor.

MagnaByte is simultaneously used with a computer and an overhead projector to project an enlarged copy of a computer screen. The viewer can see changes
in the duplication of the computer screen as they occur. MagnaByte is also
portable.

For some students, both the print on the computer screen and the print
output must be enlarged to allow full access to the computer. CCTVs are devices
that combine a camera, enlarger, and a monitor. A magnified version of whatever
is placed on the table under the camera is projected to the monitor. A student
may magnify the image from 4 to 64 times. Students may use a CCTV to read
print and to write. It has limited use in magnifying handwriting, depending on
clarity. CCTVs generally come with 14-, 16-, or 19-inch display screens (monitors) and are available with monochrome, amber, or color screens. Some CCTVs
have features that allow the user to block portions of the screen, split the screen
image for use on a computer, and display black letters on a white background or
white letters on a black background.

Figure 6-10
High resolution monitors
available to Macintosh II.
*Courtesy of Apple
Computer, Inc.*

There are several software and hardware products and combinations that combine a computer and CCTV images on the same screen. A product called Lynx projects images received through the CCTV (e.g., from a book) onto a computer monitor that simultaneously displays both the computer and CCTV images on a split screen. This allows a user to work from hard copy text while using word processing or other applications.

Other large-print programs, which are software-based, or use a combination of hardware and software to produce large-print screen output, use a mouse to manipulate the cursor and size of the display. The VISTA (TeleSensory) program is one example. ZoomText (AT Squared) is a similar software program. Some programs have the capability to work with Windows. BRAILLE-EDIT Xpress (BEX) is a self-contained program within Apple II computers that allows the user to set the print size on the screen; the number of characters on a line may vary from 5 to 80. BEX may also provide the user with the choice of voice output translation into braille and braille output.

The Macintosh computer comes standard with a program called CloseView that is used to produce larger print on the screen. inLARGE by Berkeley Systems is available for those users who need a more sophisticated screen enlargement program for the Macintosh.

Large-print paper output can be created through computers. Special codes placed in text in a word processor or other application program instruct the printer to produce the output in larger print. For example, WordPerfect 5.1 in conjunction with certain printers allows the user to set scaleable fonts to increase the print size to 20 point or greater. This is a fast and easy way to accommodate a student with low vision. It provides better clarity and contrast than enlargement with a photocopier.

Portability is a major problem with CCTV print enhancer accessibility devices. The equipment, which includes the computer and the print enhancer, takes up a considerable amount of space. The equipment is cumbersome to move, although some smaller models are available.

Braille and Other Tactual Devices. Computers can be used to produce braille materials and other raised line graphic materials. People who know very little about braille can produce braille documents with the right combination of a braille printer and braille translation software. The computer can be a teacher's aid in quickly and easily preparing handouts and testing materials. There are several braille printers on the market such as the Romeo and the Marathon (Enabling Technologies), the Braille Blazar (Blazie Engineering), and the Versa-Point (TeleSensory Inc.). The range of features in braille printers includes single versus double sided printing, adjustable paper weight and size, printing speeds, and built-in translation programs.

The computer requires a braille translation software program to produce what is called a "computer braille" file. This program translates printed text into a form that braille devices like braille printers and braille displays can understand so they can produce documents with all the appropriate contractions and abbreviations outlined in Grade II braille. Such translation programs for the IBM include Duxbury, Hot Dots, NFBTRANS, and MegaDots. The Apple II family might use a program such as BRAILLE-EDIT Xpress (BEX), which has a built-in braille translation program in addition to its editing capabilities. Some translation programs require the user to produce a document in ASCII and use embedded codes for braille formatting. Others import files from a specified word processor (such as WordPerfect) and convert the file to computer braille with appropriate formatting codes. Other programs like Megadots and BEX have built-in editors.

DEFINITION: ASCII

American Standard Code for Information Interchange. A system that assigns letters, numbers, and various other characters their own code. Information can be transferred from one computer to another via interfaces. Just because one device produces ASCII and another accepts ASCII does not mean they will operate flawlessly with one another.

Some printers have the capability of producing braille and print on the same page. The Ohtsuki braille printer prints alternating lines of braille and print on the same page. The Howtex Pixelmaster, a color thermo-jet printer, produces a similar configuration on standard paper. The Pixelmaster also has the capability of producing raised line drawings and graphics in color. Braille graphic programs such as Enabling Technologies' ETA Graphics Program produce raised line drawings on standard braille printers like the Romeo.

Braille is electronically produced though "refreshable" or "paperless" braille devices. Many of these devices are produced in either 20, 40, or 80 character displays using either 6- or 8-point dots. Paperless braille displays allow the user to review a portion of a computer screen through electrical pins, which form the corresponding braille character. The display changes as the user moves the "reading window" around the computer screen. Braille displays are helpful in explaining screen formats. An example of such a device is Navigator (TeleSensory, Inc.).

Another way of receiving tactual information through electrical impulses is to use an Optacon. An Optacon uses electrical impulses to represent the image or character seen by the camera. This device can be used to read a variety of materials, including computer screens. Berkeley systems produces a program called In-Touch, which interfaces the Optacon with images displayed on the Macintosh screen.

Optical scanners or OCRs provide for translation of print to braille, voice, or large print. Most OCRs require a computer. Kurzweil Scanning Systems are self-contained systems that will scan printed text, recognize the characters, and use

Figure 6-11
Optacon II. *Courtesy of International Business Machines Corporation.*

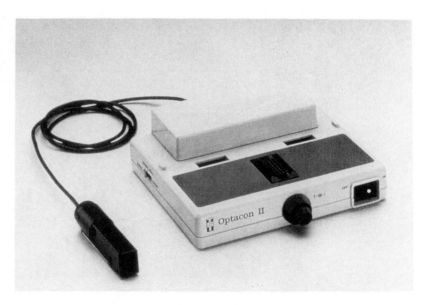

DEFINITION: Optical Character Reader (OCR)

A device that can optically analyze a printed text, recognize the letters or other characters, and store the information as a computer text file. OCRs are programmed for different styles and sizes of type and can only recognize those types.

---

this information to translate the printed text into an ASCII text file. Once the text is in ASCII form, it can be loaded from the scanner into a computer system, where it can be manipulated or displayed through some special output (synthesized voice, braille printer). The scanner can be trained to recognize virtually any type style in a document. A coprocessor card is also included to permit other applications to be carried out during scanning and recognition. Other reading systems, such as the Arkenstone Reader, use software to input text into the computer so that it can be accessed by any of the forms of adaptive technology described below. For example, textbooks not available in alternate formats can be scanned into the computer and accessed by voice output, braille display, or large-print display. Materials can be scanned through a flatbed scanner or hand-held scanner. Many commercial scanners are available at local computer stores but are not designed to be reading machines. Software allows the user to control for some

Figure 6-12
Kurzweil scanner.
Courtesy of International Business Machines Corporation.

errors made during scanning so that recognition accuracy can be improved. The quality of the original document being scanned strongly influences the quality of the scanner's recognition capability.

In addition to recognition of typewritten materials, scanners also have the ability to identify money and produce tactual drawings or pictures. Personal Data Systems (PDS) has developed software called BuckScan, which identifies denominations of paper money. Another software program, PicTax, converts scanned pictures into tactual drawings on brailled embossers.

VISION: Useful Devices/Software

Low Vision:	1. magnifiers or enlarged print
	2. highlighters
	3. adapted keyboards
	4. screen reader
Blind:	1. braille input (software-controlled)
	2. braille output
	3. screen reader
	4. Optacon
	5. Kurzweil reading device (can scan whole page)

Summary

This chapter has provided information on a number of assistive devices and how they relate to serving persons with vision disabilities. Also, the relationship between the computer—the "driver" for many of these devices—and the devices themselves was discussed.

The most important function of this chapter, however, is to set the scene for understanding the importance of assistive devices in the learning plan for the student with special needs. No device alone is sufficient to "cause" learning, but assistive devices can facilitate and embrace this learning. Teachers, supervisors, and administrators must understand the role of assistive devices in allowing the maximum development of the student with special needs in whatever areas are possible. These developmental opportunities are facilitated by computers, software, and assistive devices.

Problems of implementation, training, selection, costs, and the like, must be addressed, but all must be viewed in the context of the needs of the learner.

Assistive devices are a major support for instruction, and the future appears to be limitless when recent changes are examined. Increased technological development in the computer arena and increased understanding of the role of computers in instructional applications make the opportunities more plausible. Finally, the legal support of new laws make the possible applications more likely to occur.

References

Green, P., & Brightman, A. J. (1990). *Independence day*. Apple Computer.

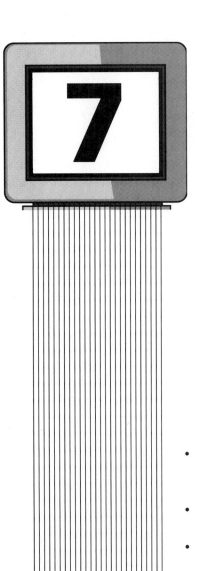

7

Assistive Devices: Hearing, Learning, Speech and Language, and Mobility

Objectives

After reading this chapter, you should be able to:

- Describe useful devices and software for students who have problems with hearing, learning, speech, and/or language and mobility.
- Define membrane keyboard; dedicated device; scanning; and toggle.
- Describe methods for keeping up with advances in adaptive technology.

As was noted in the introduction to the previous chapter, learners with special needs may require various assistive devices. This chapter deals with assistive devices for learners with specific disabilities in hearing, learning, speech and language, and mobility. We encourage the reader to be thinking in terms of how a device can also be useful to students in different disability groups.

Hearing

Persons who are deaf or hard-of-hearing present unique challenges to educators. In some types of hearing loss (conductive), amplification can be a major help while for others (sensorineural) amplification may be of little or no help. Generally, operation of a computer does not require oral communication. However, hearing loss is often coupled with a deficit in the use of the spoken and written language of the dominant culture (e.g., English), which makes the use of a computer to augment learning a viable alternative only if the students can comprehend instructions they are required to read alone. In some instances, a computer uses sound as a signaling device, in which case a light may be used to substitute for sound.

Persons with a hearing loss often use a TDD, a small portable device like a typewriter that has an acoustical coupler for the telephone receiver and a visual display or small printer to display messages. Using a TDD, a person who is deaf communicates with another person, who must also have a TDD or PhoneCommunicator. PhoneCommunicator allows communication with a touch tone phone or a TDD. Since passage of the Americans with Disabilities Act, most states now have a relay system. A deaf person using a TDD calls an operator who has a TDD. The operator places the call to a hearing person and acts as a relayer of information.

The 1310 Plus Video Communication Terminal is a telecommunication device that offers a split screen on which both conversations can be viewed simultaneously. Twenty-four lines with 40 characters are visible at one time. Monitoring the status of a call is permitted by on-screen messages (e.g., "line busy"). A built-in modem permits access to on-line databases. In addition to an automatic answering machine, which can store over 110 messages, up to 10 telephone numbers may be stored and dialed by pressing one key. Emergency information may be stored and directed to an individual with a compatible TDD. Microflip, Inc. (Silver Springs, Md.) produces a software package that allows a microcomputer with modem to act as a TDD and an answering machine. Also handy is a flashing light signaling device that lets the user who is working at the computer know he or she has a call. The user can switch to TDD mode or let the computer take and store the caller's message.

A TDD with an ASCII key, a CARR Ret key, and an ANS/ORIG switch can become a computer keyboard with the correct interface and software. This allows the TDD to be used for E-mail, which can serve to enhance the user's communication skills. Not only does a TDD (with or without E-mail) provide a teacher with access to a student's spontaneous use of written language; it also provides practice in using precise vocabulary and syntax in order to communicate exactly what the user wants to say (Pflaum, 1982).

Programs that build language and thinking skills are numerous. The ones on videodisc are a boon to students who have a hearing loss because the added visuals and sound aid comprehension in a way that printed text alone cannot do. One such videodisc is "Think It Through" (Nugent & Stone, 1982). This program shows students a dramatized situation in which a problem is presented. The students are then led through a structured decision-making process with text material. The objective is to help students develop independent thinking skills.

When teachers are previewing software they should take note of the difficulty of the linguistic structures and vocabulary the student will be required to respond to. For detailed reports on the research on technology and speech training for students who have a hearing loss, see the monograph published by the *Volta Review* (September 1989, Vol. 91, No. 5). This monograph presents studies on the use of speech training and sensory aids; computer-based speech training; and articulatory training using tactile aids. Though this research was done on subjects with hearing loss, there are possible applications for hearing students with speech problems.

Students who are deaf or hard-of-hearing can also make use of assistive software such as SpeechViewer (IBM). SpeechViewer consists of graphic displays that can be altered by the student speaking into a microphone and doing things such as raising the pitch of his or her voice, sustaining a sound, or producing a specific speech rhythm. This software is also useful for hearing students who have speech problems. (SpeechViewer is described in greater detail in the section on speech and language.) Lip Reader Trainer (Hight, 1982) is another teaching aid that uses a microcomputer. This program converts phonetic sentences into animated mouth movements. The teacher can phonetically enter sentences to be read by the student. The student watches the screen and chooses the correct sentence from four choices. This is a good tool for practice, but cannot take the place of training students in conversations with people.

Learning

We use the term *learning impairments* in a broad sense to encompass learning disabilities, cognitive impairments, and mental retardation.

Computer assistive devices for students with learning problems may allow

---

HEARING: Useful Devices/Software

Hard-of-Hearing:
1. Speech Viewer (IBM) uses an analytic rather than synthetic approach to speech development. Does not focus on auditory training (listening) skills.
2. Programs that build syntactic, semantic, pragmatic, phonology skills (expressive and receptive language)
3. Programs that build comprehension skills (HyperCard)
4. NEXT computer (videodisc)

Deaf:
1. Programs that build syntactic, semantic, pragmatic, phonology skills (expressive language and receptive language)
2. Programs that build comprehension skills (Hypercard)
3. NEXT computer (videodisc)

---

one to adapt the method of input (e.g., touch, voice), the output format (e.g.,graphics, text, audio), and the pace or speed of instruction. Another useful tool would be a program such as Co:Writer®. Co:Writer® is a word prediction program for the Macintosh for reducing keystrokes and increasing the quantity and quality of written work for people of varying abilities. "This sophisticated software ties artificial intelligence principles to individual words, the English language and the specific writer's preferences for word prediction that includes grammatically correct word choices, changing word endings, tracking favorite words and even help with sentence construction" (Don Johnson Developmental Equipment, Inc., *Co:Writer*, Wauconda, Ill.). The main dictionary shipped with Co:Writer® has more than 40,000 words. In addition, these words may be changed by adding prefixes and suffixes or by using them in new ways. Co:Writer® also learns new words and lets the writer add grammar attributes.

Generally, computer software that enhances learning and cognitive functions may be enough. However, in other instances—especially when learning impairments are coupled with physical and/or sensory impairments—other adaptive hardware or software may be needed for computer access. In this area, the ability of the computer to support a multisensory approach is of major importance. This allows for *visual* cues through graphics and animation, *auditory* cues through music, voice, and sound prompts, and *tactile* cues through the keyboard or touch screen.

LEARNING: Useful Devices/Software

1. word prediction programs
2. outliners
3. programs that allow variable spacing, highlighting, color change
4. See chapter on vision for magnifiers, speech synthesizers, and enlarged print that may help

Speech and Language

In the area of speech and language disorders, the user may have some type of articulation problem, delayed speech development, impairment of language function, or any of a wide range of disorders.

The IBM Personal System/2 SpeechViewer

The IBM SpeechViewer is a compact clinical tool designed to increase the efficiency of speech therapy. It uses the IBM Personal System/2 computer to convert elements of speech acoustics into interactive graphic displays that are synchronized with digital audio playback. Moveable visual symbols enable clinicians to demonstrate to clients key features of speech models and feedback.

Figure 7-1
SpeechViewer. *Courtesy of International Business Machines Corporation.*

A group of 12 clinical modules is designed to complement the clinician's therapy methods. SpeechViewer allows the clinician to present speech stimuli visually, and gives clients feedback to each response.

SpeechViewer Components

SpeechViewer runs with the IBM Personal System/2 Model 25, Model 30, or Model 30 286 computers. It is a combination of hardware, software, and supportive documentation. Hardware consists of a microphone, a speaker, and a speech analysis adapter case that plugs into a full-size expansion slot of the PS/2 computer. SpeechViewer application software consists of 13 program modules that address a wide variety of speech attributes. These modules enable the input, digitation, storage, and analysis of speech, in addition to real-time speech display and playback.

Speech Digitizer

A speech digitizer is a device that analyzes speech and converts particular sounds or utterances into digital patterns that may be stored on a computer the same as other data. These digital patterns can be reconverted into their original sounds. Speech digitizers are also used in voice recognition systems.

Speech Synthesizer

In contrast to the speech digitizer, which records and plays back what it "hears", the speech synthesizer receives input in the form of electronic characters (e.g., letters, numbers) and converts the characters into artificial speech. Although it uses less memory, the synthesizer produces a sound that is more mechanical than that of a digitizer. Every phrase does not have to be spoken with a synthesizer because most have a memory and processing system that applies standard pronunciation rules to determine the correct pronunciation.

This type of assistive device, connected to a computer or incorporated into the software, is used in teaching or training the person who is speech impaired or as a voice output for the nonvocal person. There are other devices for the person who is nonvocal or speech impaired and who also has a mobility impairment (see the following section).

DynaVox

The DynaVox is a communication aid that offers people with speech disabilities empowerment because it makes it easy for them to create an unlimited range of personal messages, and speak them electronically with a simple touch. Almost anyone can begin using it in less than half an hour.

The DynaVox also gives personalized voice output with DECtalk™ technology (Digital Equipment Corporation). It offers 10 different voices, ranging from child to adult in both male and female voice tones.

Figure 7-2
DynaVox: Used by
persons with speech
disabilities to speak
electronically. *Courtesy
of Sentient Systems
Technology Inc.*

Liberator

Liberator is a communication tool available to nonspeaking persons. In addition to offering speech synthesis, it is a writing tool that can also be used as an alternate keyboard to most computers and can operate an environmental control.

COMMUNICATION: Useful Devices/Software

Language:
1. Mayer-Johnson (MAC) by Terri Johnson
2. PEAL (Programs for Early Acquisition of Language) Apple by Laura Meyers
3. Word processing (with or without speech synthesizer) —with speech for children who are poor readers

Speech:
1. Stand-alone communication devices (e.g., DynaVox digitized speech; animated graphics)
2. SpeechViewer (IBM)

Figure 7-3
Liberator. *Courtesy of
Prentke Romich
Company.*

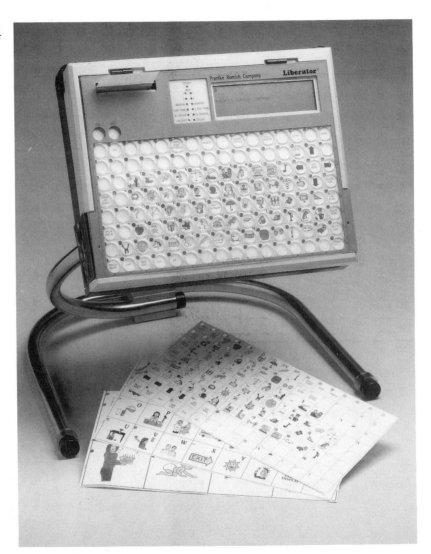

Mobility

Mobility issues related to computer usage are of course directly related to the severity and type of mobility problem. Basic considerations include the degree of mobility impairment, positioning, endurance, and communication. Several examples of assistive devices follow.

HeadMaster

HeadMaster allows persons who are unable to use their hands to operate a computer. It achieves this by taking the place of the mouse. As you move your head, the headset and control unit work together to measure the rotation of your head and move the cursor on the screen. Activation of the attached puff switch (one puffs into a straw-like device) or other control interface makes the selection.

For typing and other keyboard functions, on-screen keyboard programs put a picture of a keyboard on the screen that the HeadMaster can activate. A new remote version eliminates the connection between the headset and the computer, allowing the user to come and go without removing the headset.

As stated before, the HeadMaster is a mouse emulator that is controlled with the head. A control unit sends out an ultrasonic signal, which is picked up by three receivers in the headset. The control unit and headset then work together to triangulate the head's position and translate its movement into cursor movement on the screen. Activating a puff switch makes selections. Software programs that put an image of a keyboard on the display permit full keyboard operation.

Ke:nx On:Board

Ke:nx On:Board (pronounced "connects") is a membrane keyboard made especially for the Macintosh computer. The complete Ke:nx On:Board includes everything needed for use with the Macintosh PowerBooks, LCs, and other models. Extra overlays are available as well as customization software for making and printing new overlays in color or in black and white. Speech capabilities allow users to make "talking" keys. Ke:nx On:Board has a flat surface. Areas of the surface are formed into extralarge keys. Large letters are printed on large keys.

Figure 7-4
Headmaster with Sip
and Puff Switch.
*Courtesy of Prentke
Romich Company.*

Graphics show special functions. Keyboard keys are adjustable to accommodate both those with a feather-light press and those who are on the heavy-handed side. The Shift, Command, Option, and Control keys work sequentially with other keys, replacing simultaneous keystroke requirements.

Extra keyboard overlays and setups are available that allow a user to change the keyboard look and function instantly. Available are black letters printed on a white background, a mouse overlay for drawing or education programs, a large numbers overlay, and a colorful alphabetical order overlay with numbers and arrows for younger users.

DEFINITION: Membrane Keyboard

A keyboard whose keys are located under a flexible surface with no openings. The student activates the keys by pressing on the membrane.

Ke:nx

Ke:nx is an alternate access system for use with the Macintosh for people with physical or cognitive limitations due to disability or injury. Ke:nx lets the user have alternate input devices such as switches or expanded keyboards to take charge of every aspect of computer operation.

Ke:nx is invisible to other software so Macintosh programs look and act as if the regular keyboard and mouse were used instead of an input method. It is possible to use a Ke:nx input method to operate all standard software, including word processors, spreadsheets, database, games, and utilities. New input methods are Ke:nx OnScreen, auditory scanning, and a method for connecting a dedicated communication device to the keyboard. Other input methods are single switch scanning, Morse code, expanded or mini keyboards, and assisted keyboards. Each input is adjustable to individual user's needs.

DEFINITION: Dedicated Device

A device that cannot be shared among users. Designed to perform one task, a dedicated device is capable of performing one and only one function at a time.

With mobility sometimes being a problem, a wheelchair computer cubical offers accessibility and privacy to the students. The mobility of the cubical makes it even easier to adapt to the student's needs.

DEFINITION: Scanning

Scanning involves moving through a given set of choices, and making a selection when the correct position is found. There are different types of scanning, which include automatic, manual, row and column, and directed. In automatic scanning, the system scans automatically once started, and the user activates a switch to stop the scanning. In manual scanning, the individual activates a switch to scan the choices, releasing the switch to stop. In row and column scanning, the individual selects the row in a grid first, then the column. In direct scanning, multiple switches or a joystick is used to scan in the correct direction.

Touch Talker Accessing an Apple IIe

For years the Touch Talker and Light Talker were the standard against which all other communication devices were measured. The Light Talker is a communication aid with synthesized speech output and optional printer or keyboard. Selection can be direct with a head pointer or scanning with switches. Morse code input is also possible. The Light Talker has the same features as the Touch Talker

Figure 7-6
Computer cart accessible
by wheelchair. *Courtesy
of Fred Sammons Inc.*

except that it has been designed for persons who cannot activate a standard keyboard. It offers 25 different selection techniques. The Touch Talker is similar but comes with a membrane keyboard. Both can be used to operate a computer. They remain powerful tools with the inclusion of an Enhanced Minispeak Operating System (EMOS), which includes error keys, additional storage, and extra work space.

Modifications and Alternatives to Standard Keyboards

Persons with limited motor control or persons using a headstick or mouthstick often use these items.

- A keyguard is a keyboard overlay with holes positioned over each key. This assists in stabilization of finger, hand, or stick movement. A single-finger

Figure 7-7
Ke:nx, Mouse alternative
interface. *Courtesy of
Don Johnston
Developmental Equip.
Inc.*

Figure 7-8
Touch Talker. *Courtesy of
Prentke Romich
Company.*

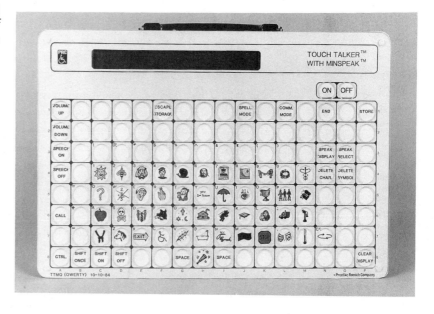

Figure 7-9
Key Largo, a membrane keyboard. *Courtesy of Don Johnston Developmental Equip. Inc.*

software program allows the user to modify keys such as Shift so that two or more keys need not be depressed simultaneously.

- A keylatcher may be used to lock specific keys.
- Membrane keyboards can be used by individuals who can work at a flat service, but not depress a key. Key Largo (Figure 7-9) is an example of a membrane keyboard.
- Expanded keyboards are for persons who can use only a large area or, in the opposite case, have extremely limited range of motion and/or movement of their limbs. The large area enables a person without use of arms to access the computer with the feet. Similarly, an individual who may have difficulty hitting the small keys will find it much easier to manipulate the extralarge keys. Expanded keyboards are of help to people who need to use a computer in bed or from a wheelchair because they usually attach to the computer with a long, thin cable.
- A touch screen mounts to most 10- to 15-inch monitors. It allows interaction with a computer by touching the screen rather than by using a keyboard or switch. It can also be used as a graphics tablet.
- A touch pads is a continuous membrane surface divided into areas, each of which generates a different input. Touch pads are usually used to make selections from menus.
- An oral keyboard is an alternative keyboard used to provide input to computers and electronic typewriters. The student "sips" on a mouthpiece to control cursor scanning of a small electronic display that sits on the top of a computer. The rate of scanning is controlled by the amount

Figure 7-10
Touch Window, a touch
screen. *Courtesy of Fred
Sammons Inc.*

of pressure applied in sipping. When the cursor is over the desired character,
puffing into the mouthpiece selects that character.

Keyports

Items, reminiscent of keyboards, which can help reduce typing are illustrated by
the Keyport 60 and the Keyport 300; both developed by Polytel. These products
are not designed specifically for people with disabilities, but can prove quite
useful. Both are flat membrane keypads with several overlay sheets that can be
changed for different sets of functions. They are meant to supplement, not
replace, the computer's standard keyboard. Each key can be programmed on
these touch pads to enter a large number of keystrokes when depressed once and
thus save typing. A commonly used word or phrase or arithmetic operation may
be programmed. The Keyport 60 has 60 user-definable ports and rests above the
standard keyboard; the 300 has 300 places and lies alongside the keyboard. They
work with IBM PC, XT, AT jr., and true compatibles.

MOBILITY: Useful Devices/Software

1. switches for computer and environmental controls
2. adapted keyboards
3. key guards

Figure 7-11
Keyport 60. *Courtesy of Polytel Computer Products.*

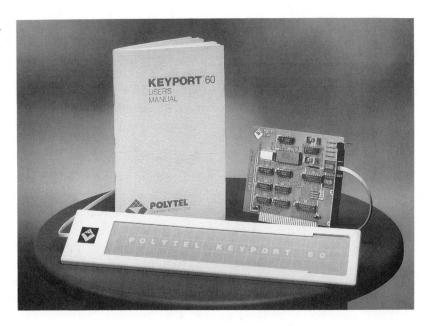

Figure 7-12
Keyport 300, A keyboard supplement with 300 definable ports. *Courtesy of Polytel Computer Products.*

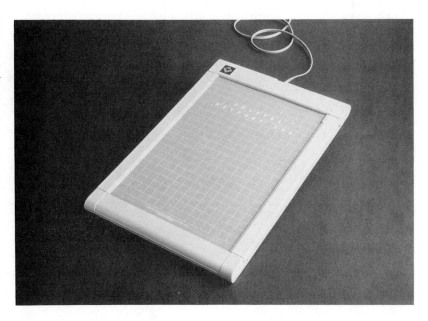

Alternative Input Methods

There are three broad categories of alternative input methods. *Switches* can be activated by almost any motion, by almost any part of the body. Switches can be activated, for example, by touching with a finger, wrinkling the forehead, raising an eyebrow, or pushing with a big toe. They can be tedious and time-consuming but incredibly helpful to someone who might only be able to move an eyebrow up or down. Scanning and mouse work entry are two applications of the switch to gain access to computers.

Direct selection is any technique for selecting choices that allows the user to point to target items using a single action such as eye gaze, head pointer, or light beam. This contrasts with scanning, in which choices are offered sequentially and the student signals when the desired selection is reached.

Voice recognition is an alternate input method by which a computer accepts a spoken command. Voice recognition recognizes an utterance by digitally encoding it once or several times. Thereafter when it "hears" an utterance, it compares it to the patterns for the utterances "heard" before, and matches it to one. For example, DragonDictate-30K is a speech recognition system. It consists of a software program and a peripheral card that plugs into a PC. This system provides the capability to create text and operate a computer by speaking. PC users who can't type or whose hands are busy can create memos, reports, spreadsheets, novels—any free text—by speaking instead of typing. The computer matches voice commands against a stored voice pattern. Voice recognition systems hold

Figure 7-13
Grasp switch for persons with limited coordination. *Courtesy of International Business Machines Corporation.*

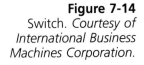

Figure 7-14
Switch. *Courtesy of
International Business
Machines Corporation.*

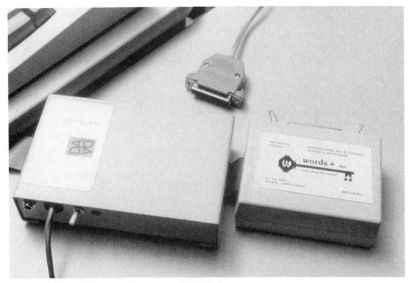

immense potential for persons with movement limitations; they effectively regu-
late the computer without any physical interaction between the person and
computer. Following are specific examples of the alternative input methods.

The *grasp switch* may be used by a person with limited coordination. Squeez-
ing the hand-held or foot-pressured device operates the workstation. All switches
attach to the workstation via adapters connected to the serial or parallel port.
Figures 7-13 and 7-14 show sample devices that allow the attachment of a variety
of switches or alternative keyboards. They attach externally to the serial or parallel ports of a PC. Each has an associated software interface program for flexibility
in attaching devices.

A *puff switch* is a switch activated by puffing into a mouthpiece attached to a
tube. It requires only minimal breath (.1018 PSI) to activate single switch programs. It mounts to a table, tray, or wheelchair and has a bendable gooseneck for
positions comfortable for the user.

An *eyebrow switch* is mounted on a visor. A lever projects down in front of
the forehead, resting against it. When the user wrinkles the forehead or raises an
eyebrow, the switch is activated with a clicking sound.

A *computer keyboard switch* is a small version of a computer keyboard that
functions as a single switch. Pressing a key activates a function and pressing the
same key stops the process.

Environmental controls are devices or systems whose function is to control
some other device in the person's environment. These devices help an individual
operate lights, radio, television, or telephone.

Figure 7-15
Puff switch. *Courtesy of Fred Sammons Inc.*

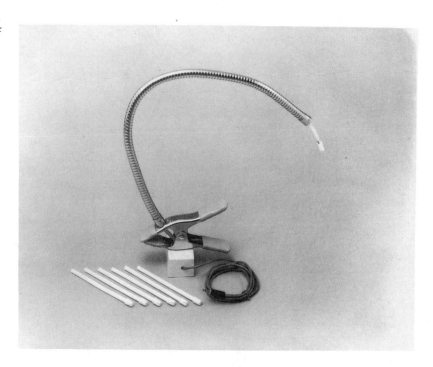

A person with a disability that affects the muscles used in speaking may need to use *electronic communication aids* providing synthesized speech or written output.

For the person who can control only eye muscles an entirely different set of accommodations is sought. There is technology available that allows a camera to be attached to a person's head, facing the emulator screen, which displays a keyboard. The camera sends an image of the screen to the emulator, which displays a dot at the spot to which the user is turned. If a gaze is held for a second, the selected letter appears on the screen of the machine. Additional devices allow a user to wear a lightweight reflector on the head or any part of the body that sends an infrared signal indicating where the cursor should go.

For those with greater muscular control, lower-tech options are available. People with good control of their neck and head muscles, for example, can use a mouthstick, which is a piece of wood or plastic with a "U"-shaped end that the user grips between the teeth to jab at the keyboard. Mouthsticks are inexpensive; sometimes even an ordinary pencil will suffice. A mouthstick user can become almost as proficient as a one-finger typist. The head pointer is an adjustable headset with a rubber-tipped stick that extends from the forehead. The individual positions his or her head over the keyboard and jabs at the keys desired.

Figure 7-16
Mouthstick. *Courtesy of
Fred Sammons Inc.*

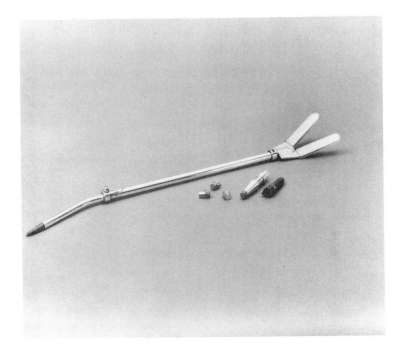

Many persons who have quadriplegia or cerebral palsy lack the neck-muscle control the device demands. And there are other complications: the stick must be kept clean because it sits so long in the user's mouth, and the keyboard must be shielded from saliva. Also, it is impossible to depress two keys simultaneously.

The mini keyboard measures 4 by 7 inches and is used by persons with minimum vertical and lateral hand movement capability. This keyboard is programmable to allow rearrangement of the keys if required.

Keyboard macro programs let the user modify the keyboard to combine common commands into a single keystroke. Such software also turns the Alt, Ctrl, and Shift keys into toggle switches—press once to activate, a second time to

---

DEFINITION: Toggle

A switching action where the switch is turned on with one motion, and off with another. The switch remains on or off only while it is being activated by the user. A common toggle switch is a wall switch for a light. This is also known as latching.

Figure 7-17
Mini-keyboard. *Courtesy of International Business Machines Corporation.*

deactivate. For a nondisabled PC user, such macros represent power tools; for the person who has a disability, they are a necessity.

Other help comes in the form of simple devices such as keyguards. These let people with poor arm control rest their hands on the keyboard without making accidental keystrokes. To push a key they must poke a finger or stick through a hole in the protective shield.

Keyguard

A keyguard is a piece of plastic with holes drilled directly above each key. It fits over the standard keyboard to prevent users from making accidental contact with the keys. To strike a key a person with a tremor or spastic hand movement, or who might use a mouth or head pointer, can go directly to one key without hitting several keys in the process. Since many persons who would find this type of device useful might also have difficulty pressing more than one key at the same time, a number of keyguards come fitted with keylatches. Keylatches attach to the keyboard and are activated by sliding a metal or plastic object over the key(s) that need to be held down. Computer software sometimes requires that two or three keys be held down at the same time. Such keys as Command, Shift, and Option are the most commonly used keys.

Key Repeat Eliminators

Most keyboards allow users to repeat any character simply by holding down the key. When the key is released, the repeating halts. This can be a convenient feature

Figure 7-18
Keyguard. *Courtesy of International Business Machines Corporation.*

for someone who wants to type a row of one character (e.g., dashes). For a student using a pointer or mouthstick or who has motor difficulties, this feature can present a real problem. The screen has unwanted characters because the mouthstick, finger, or pointer unintentionally held the key down too long. Some computers have a built-in program that manages the rate at which the key will repeat. For computers without this feature a small device called a key repeat eliminator effectively shuts off the repeating feature. An on/off switch that can be mounted outside the computer's housing is installed so that normal keyboard operations for typing are possible.

Specialty keyboards can also compensate for specific disabilities. Those with cerebral palsy who can make large arm movements but lack fine motor control, for example, can use an oversized keyboard device. Additionally, a mini keyboard is designed for people with good dexterity but limited range of motion, such as those who have muscular dystrophy. A PowerPad (Figure 6-7) has a programmable surface keyboard and provides a durable large "target" option for a person with limited hand coordination.

Keyboard Mouse

With a keyboard mouse a user can control every feature of the standard mouse from the numeric pad of the keyboard. Pressing the "8" key makes the mouse cursor move up, pressing the "6" key makes it slide to the right. A user can simulate every function of the standard mouse in this manner. The rate of the pointer is adjustable from the computer's keyboard.

Figure 7-19
Keylatch. *Courtesy of
Fred Sammons Inc.*

Figure 7-19
Keylatch. *Courtesy of Fred Sammons Inc.*

Joysticks and Trackballs

A joystick is often an ideal alternative to the mouse because it can be placed in unique places and activated with different parts of the body (e.g., the chin and the mouth). A trackball is a device for people who do not have a wide range of movement in their arms and hands. Joysticks and trackballs stay in one area and do not need to be moved across the tabletop.

Disk Guides and Hooks

Disk guides provide a stable surface for people with poor hand control to align the disk with the drive opening. Made of durable kydex, they mount securely with dual lock. Disk hooks make it easier for a computer user to insert or remove floppy disks with a mouthstick or a head pointer.

PC devices, mostly from small, single-focus companies, are helping PC users with disabilities overcome physical handicaps. For example, computers can talk to those who are blind and listen to the commands of those who cannot move. Head-mounted switches and other devices let persons with severe paralysis use Morse code to communicate with the PC and therefore other people. The PC can introduce those with disabilities to people, activities, and opportunities that they could not otherwise enjoy.

Figure 7-20
Joystick. *Courtesy of Prentke Romich Company.*

Figure 7-21
Trackball. *Courtesy of Kensington Microwave Limited.*

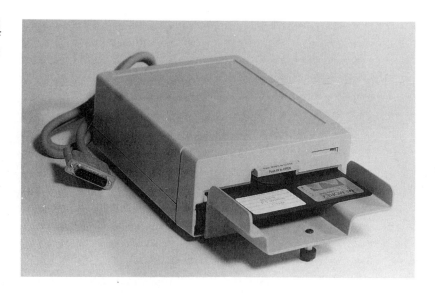

New Areas

New, more exotic technologies for persons with disabilities promise even better results in the foreseeable future. PRAB Command in Kalamazoo, Michigan, has adapted one of its robot systems to fulfill the far more delicate mission of office servant. The robot is fully voice-controlled. The user can say, "Get Lotus," for example, and the arm fetches the 1–2-3 manual from a bin. Say "Get drink," and the mechanical servant brings a container of water.

A brain-wave interface developed at the Smith-Kettlewell Eye Research Institute in San Francisco can monitor electrical activity in the brain to find out where on the screen the user is staring. The trick is to divide the display into a checkerboard, with each square flashing on and off at different intervals. The interface is able to determine which section of the screen is being looked at by reading the user's brain waves, which pulsate in synchrony with the part of the screen being viewed.

Researchers elsewhere are taking the brain-scanning idea one step further, according to Mary Pat Radabaugh, director of the IBM National Support Center for Persons with Disabilities, in Atlanta, Georgia. The premise is that people's brains respond to words and ideas in similar ways. Two different people who think about "trees," for example, might produce similar patterns of electrical activity in their brains. The objective is to calibrate a computer input to the pattern. Then a user could strap on some electrodes and think about "trees," and the word *trees* (or a picture) would appear on screen.

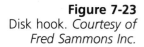
Figure 7-23
Disk hook. *Courtesy of Fred Sammons Inc.*

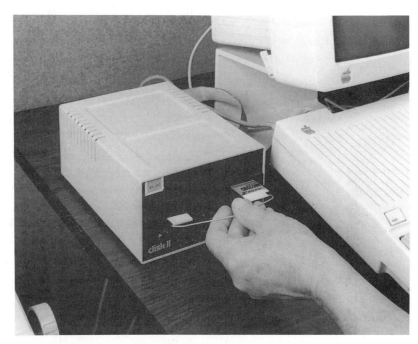

How to Keep Up With Advances in Adaptive Technology

Keeping up with advances in technology can be a daunting task. There are more publications on adaptive technology than a teacher has time to read. Figure 7-24 presents a partial list of publications that will be useful. Often the school librarian will be keeping up with the latest developments. A journal, *Computers in Libraries*, has a section called "adaptive technology." This section is one or two pages of summaries about the latest innovations. Each summary includes telephone numbers and addresses of the companies producing the products. Someone in the school should be designated as the person responsible for keeping abreast of this information. (Appendix J provides names and information of organizations and agencies helpful to persons with disabilities.)

Summary

This chapter, paralleling Chapter 6, has provided information and a number of assistive devices and how they can serve persons with disabilities in the areas of hearing, learning, speech and language, and mobility. As was noted in Chapter 6,

Figure 7-24
Where to subscribe.
Source: Computes in
Libraries, April, 1993,
Vol. 13, No. 4.

WHERE TO SUBSCRIBE	
Closing the Gap: Closing the Gap P.O. Box 68 Henderson, MN 56044 Cost: $26 (6 issues)	*Link-Up:* The National Library of Australia Parkes Place Canberra ACT 2600 Disability Services Section Cost: free (6 issues)
Computer Disability News: Computer Disability News National Easter Seal Society 70 E. Lake Street Chicago, IL 60602 Cost: free (4 issues)	*SAF Technology Update:* Sensory Access Foundation 385 Sherman Avenue, Suite 2 Palo Alto, CA 94306 Cost: $47 for organizations (6 issues). Inquire for other pricing schemes.
Focus: Michael G. Gunde 216 N. Frederick Avenue Daytona Beach, FL 32114 Cost: $12 (12 issues U.S.)	*Tactic:* Clovernook Printing House for the Blind 700 Hamilton Avenue Cincinnati, OH 45231 Cost $20 (4 issues, large print or braille)
GA-SK Newsletter: TDI 8719 Colesville Road #300 Silver Springs, MD 20910 Cost: $15 (4 issues)	Where to write for membership applications or more information about the American Library Association ASCLA Division or LITA Division or LAMA Division of American Library Association 50 East Huron Road Chicago, IL 60611 (800) 545-2433

(*continued*)

Figure 7-24
(*Continued*)

WHERE TO SUBSCRIBE	
In the Mainstream: Mainstream 3 Bethesda Boulevard Bethesda, MD 20814 Write for subscription as this newsletter is moving from newsletter format to journal format.	
Library Access: Institute for the Study of Developmental Disabilities 2853 East Tenth Street Bloomington, IN 47405 Cost: $10 (4 issues)	

the emphasis is on how these devices facilitate learning, rather than how the devices work.

Again, the authors see these devices as support for and suggestions for the instructional program.

References

Don Johnson Developmental Equipment. (1990). *Co:Writer.* Wauconda, IL: Don Johnson Developmental Equipment.

Hight, R. L. (1982). Lip reader trainer: Teaching aid for the hearing impaired. *American Annals of the Deaf, 127,* 564–568.

Nugent, G. C., & Stone, C. G. (1982). The videodisc meets the microcomputer. *American Annals of the Deaf, 127* (5), 569–572.

Pflaum, M. B. (1982). The California connections: Interfacing a telecommunication devices for the deaf (TDD) and on an Apple computer. *American Annals of the Deaf, 127,* 573–584.

McGarr, N. S. (Ed.). (1989). Research on the use of sensory aids for hearing-impaired people [Special issue]. *Volta Review, 91* (5).

8

Where To: The Future

Objectives

After reading this chapter, you should be able to:

- Describe economic considerations with regard to providing technological assistance to learners with special needs.
- Discuss societal factors, specifically the impact of educational reform, on technology in the schools.
- Describe equity issues in computer use affecting the schools.
- Describe ways to augment school staff.

Minority students, gifted students, residential students in special schools, and a number of other groups vie for the allocation of scarce resources. It is impossible to rank or prioritize these groups, but following are factors that have impact on the direction of programs and opportunities for learners with special needs. Discussions in this chapter are divided into technological and nontechnological areas. Clearly both impact the future of learners with special needs. Each is related to the other, but each is also an independent area of concern.

Technological Issues

Of concern to learners with special needs, parents, and professionals is the continued development of more sophisticated, more expensive equipment and more utilitarian, usable software. While it may seem strange to equate positive growth with problems, the troublesome issues are the cost and complexity of new items and the obsolescence of older equipment. More often than not, the increased utility or usability of a new piece of hardware or a new software product means increased costs and required procedural changes for personnel. Additionally, many times the introduction of an item of hardware causes persons to suggest replacing items or altering procedures that are currently working well. If however, the IEP requires a *particular* piece of hardware or software package for implementation, the district has no option. In reality, the programmatic impact of the new "bells and whistles" may be superficial rather than substantive. Additionally the "Keeping up with the Jones" syndrome can result in the spending of scarce resources unwisely. In some instances, older and less sophisticated equipment can be moved to other school programs or areas where appropriate and effective applications are possible; equipment—except when maintenance and repair costs exceed value—continues to have some utility for many, varied program applications. Site-based budgeting can affect decisions to a degree, but many school districts will continue to deal with programs and procedures for learners with special needs from the central office at the district level. This structure is really a mixed blessing. Economies of scale suggest purchasing power from the top, but program needs and student support can often be much more effectively accomplished with decisions made by local site personnel.

Overall, the economic conditions relative to school settings are not bright. Continued budget shortfalls in many states and cities and reduced federal aid do not bode well for short-term improvement. Economic impact also is felt by the many state and federal laws or mandates for which no funds for implementation are provided. Equipment purchases often rank just above roof repair and boiler replacements and well below salaries, staff development appropriations, and supplies/textbook expenditures. Additionally, even though computer hardware and software costs are down, the opportunities for uses and needs for additional special assistive devices continue to grow. As more needs are identified, these areas will require even more funding. The selection or authorization of who makes program decisions continues to be key for learners with special needs. Without belaboring the point, these students are at the mercy of the site and district administrative staff, school boards and state budget officers. One final note (perhaps a truly bright light): there continues to be *some* laws that require the provision of certain services that may require certain types of hardware and specific software packages. The down side of this lies in the actual implementation and the necessary legal support to be certain that all provisions of the law are enforced. Additionally, funding continues to be a major issue.

Finally, it should be remembered that technological advances are often a mixed blessing. Increased applications for software and hardware create expectations that often cannot be met or can only be met at high costs in personnel, training, and equipment/software support. Much remains to be done to effectively integrate technology with educational needs and opportunities—especially the needs and opportunities of the special learner.

Systems Integration

There is little argument that the need to integrate all factors—hardware, software, and personnel—into one system is the most efficient way to proceed with computer applications for instruction. The concept of integration allows for a total systems approach to the solution of problems and thus provides the reachable goal of delivery of the best educational opportunity in the least restrictive environment for the most reasonable cost possible. It really is a myth that what needs to happen or rather what *must* be done always can be done in an inexpensive manner. There are times that what needs to be done must be done, without major consideration for cost factors!

Success of a systems integration approach rests on a number of issues, the most important, if not the most desirable, being cost considerations. As envisioned in this text the integration is within the classroom or school and includes the pupil, a basic computer system, appropriate assistive devices, necessary software, and teacher, parent, administrator, and community involvement and support. Finally, the learner with special needs becomes an integrated part of the total learning environment and is not separated or isolated from the total school program.

Societal Factors

Funding/Cost Effectiveness

Key to the continued development and usage of integrated systems—hardware, software, and personnel—is the major issue of cost. Cost is often a more important consideration than development of new machines, introduction of major software systems, or the emergence of a better trained, more caring professional staff. The selection/implementation of any new program is really dependent on the availability of funding. Even the emergence of the most cost-effective measures is not able to turn a limited budget allocation into a larger one. School personnel and school boards are faced with an often reluctant public's willingness to fund an ever-growing school budget—whether at the state or local level. Concerns with a lack of productivity and depressed graduation rates and measures of student performance have contributed to a wary public's concerns— especially related to increased budget requests.

With this wariness comes the opportunity for schools and systems to be more creative in securing funds from nontraditional sources. The use of corporate sponsors and such programs as Adopt-a-School allow systems and sites to tap sources of funds not related to the general tax base of an area. Again, the school or district needs to have something to offer. Program goals must be well defined, structures for implementation should be in place, and performance objectives should be stated. Knowing what is needed and how positive results will be affected is a key point in selling to corporate sponsors.

Even spectacular developments or improvements in hardware, software, and/ or adaptive devices likely will not be embraced until budget situations become more flexible. A final cost/funding consideration also may relate to specialized training or staff development costs associated with the use, implementation, and maintenance of hardware and software applications.

Educational Reform

Educational reform—viewed as a major, positive direction for most schools— may prove to be an enemy of the student with special needs. If the energies and resources of the nation are spent reorganizing and reforming schools, then for the short run instructional change will be caught up in the needs for new organizational structures, new instructional plans, and new curricular initiatives. All such efforts support improved instruction; however, actual, day-to-day improvement, especially for subpopulations such as learners with special needs, often follows much later. Additionally, the learning environment of many students with special needs is fragile at best. Disruptions and uncertainty in this environment often are negative influences. The development of support groups and positive learner environments need to be maintained.

Ideas like the voucher plan and school restructuring development efforts such as the Whittle Communications' Edison Project may provide a positive, long-range impact on the solutions of the myriad problems facing schools; however, the short-range effect must be carefully observed and monitored. In some selected activities, due to cost considerations and a need to fully understand the new structure, the learner with special needs is often the last student to be factored into the equation. Educators need to dream, but reality relative to delivery of services often must be faced.

Acceptance

While not a topic often discussed, the issue of acceptance of learners with special needs continues to be a concern to parents, school professionals, and the students themselves. The issue is one not only of acceptance of the individual student but an acceptance of the expenditure of such a large (perceived or real) sum for the purchase of hardware, software, and assistive devices for a single student. In systems and schools where basic supplies, including textbooks, are in short supply or nonexistent, the cost of providing necessary services to one student—even though required by law—is not seen in a positive light because most people don't realize that special education funds are a separate category. Funds are not taken from the regular program to serve students with special needs. While empathy is present for these learners, the difficulty of overcoming budgetary shortfalls is often difficult. Care must be exercised in establishing the need for and implementation of such services. Changes in legal definitions of students with special needs and expanded opportunities must always be considered in any decisions.

Human Factors

Equity Issues in Computer Use in Schools

While technology advances daily, the world of education is slow to change. There are enormous amounts of money being spent for technological research and development, while almost everything in education is underfunded. Technology, specifically computer technology, is expensive—though less now and projected to go even lower. The cost of hardware, for example, has declined dramatically over the past few years, but the need for *more* workstations and more and improved adaptive devices has kept the total costs from dropping sharply. Logic tells us that more affluent public schools will have more access to computers than poor schools; and in fact, this is the case. Students from more affluent schools have a higher probability of achieving in postsecondary programs than students from less affluent schools. Add access to technology to this equation and the gap between students in the two schools grows even wider.

Sutton (1991) summarized the 1980s research conducted on race/ethnicity, gender, and social class differences in K–12 educational use of computers. Researchers found that inequalities do exist within and among schools. Equity issues in school computer use are important for economic and moral reasons. We've mentioned the differences that exist between "poor" schools and "rich" schools. Add to this the fact that children with disabilities are in all schools and the picture becomes even more complicated. As a matter of fact (and law) the increased integration of students with special needs into the regular program of a school is an increasing likelihood.

The rest of this section includes selected results from Sutton's (1991) review of research. We choose our examples in hopes that they shift teachers into an equity mind-set. Much of the racism, sexism, and classism perpetuated by teachers is inadvertent. If teachers are aware of some specific ways inequities are perpetuated, they will be more likely to avoid them.

Access

Poor and minority children have less access to computers at home and at school. Researchers found that high school students whose parents had graduated from college were three times more likely to own computers than high school students whose parents had not graduated from college.

Generally males have more access to computers than females and males are more likely to attend computer camps. The review of research also found that families with male children are more likely to own computers.

Type of Use

Poor and minority students spend more time on drill and practice and less time on programming than high socioeconomic status (SES) white students. This means that poor and minority students interact with computers where computers are in control, while high SES students work in situations where they are in control of the computer. Females are less likely to participate in game playing, before and after school use, and elective programming classes. Females also are overrepresented in word-processing classes.

Attitudes

In general many teachers believe that good behavior should be rewarded with time using the computer and that low-achieving students should use computers for drill and practice (basic skills) activities only. Photographs in textbooks and magazines often portray computer use as a white male activity. Boys may perceive computer use as a male domain. Positive attitudes toward computers correlate with experience with computers, and white middle-class males have more experience.

In essence, students who are poor, female, minority, or low-achieving are likely to be further behind after computers are introduced into a school. Changes in this pattern are slow in coming, but improvement has begun.

Helping Personnel

Educational systems often believe they are understaffed and underfunded. A way that some schools cope with these problems is extensive use of noncertified and/or volunteer personnel. By establishing liaisons with service organizations and parent groups, teachers can bring personnel into their classrooms and with minimal training make use of the volunteers' skills. If volunteers have few or no computer skills they may want to learn them. Volunteers can work cooperatively to learn how to use specific software. Another source of possible valuable assistance is a peer tutoring program involving students in other grades at a given site or from other sites. Once volunteers (and students) are familiar with computers, their confidence in their abilities to try new things increases. With volunteers in the classroom teachers must be organized. Planning will take more teacher time but the payoff should be worth it.

Students with disabilities who have computer skills could be asked to teach students who are less skilled. The parents of children with disabilities who make constant use of computer assistive devices could be an excellent resource in a classroom either for a short time or on a regular schedule.

Teachers need to seek out community resources; they need to talk to parents, grandparents, other family members. The more communities are involved in their schools, the more the students will gain. The authors note the appropriate responsibilities for teachers (and administrators), but the long term payoff generally is well worth the investment.

The Next Efforts

The future of education for the learner with special needs continues to hold great promise—tempered with the harsh realities of economics, apathy, fear, and disinterest and resistance to change. The technology is in place to do much more than is being done, and the technology continues to advance. The public's—including educators'—legal, ethical, and moral ability to cope with many of these advances is yet to be determined.

More opportunities are available than can be seen, but the quest for success continues to be elusive.

References

Sutton, R. E. (1991). Equity and computers in the schools: A decade of research. *Review of Educational Research, 61*, 475–503.

APPENDIX A
Litigation and Legislation

The following is a summary of important litigation and legislation affecting special education taken from G. P. Cartwright, C. A. Cartwright, & M E. Ward. (1989). *Educating special learners* (3d ed.). Belmont, Calif.: Wadsworth Publishing Co., pp. 21–22.

Litigation

1. **Brown v. Board of Education of Topeka, Kansas.** 347 U.S. 483 (1954). It was alleged that separate educational facilities for black students violated their rights under the Fourteenth Amendment of the U.S. Constitution. The plaintiffs felt it was unlawful to discriminate against a class of persons for an arbitrary or unjustifiable reason.

2. **Diana v. [California] State Board of Education.** C-70 37 PFR (1970). Nine Mexican-American public school students ages eight through 13 alleged that they had been inappropriately placed in classes for students with retardation on the basis of biased, standardized intelligence tests. The plaintiffs came from home environments in which Spanish was the only or predominant language spoken.

3. **Wyatt v. Aderholt.** 334 F Supp. 1341 (1971) (originally Wyatt v. Stickney). It was alleged that the two Alabama state mental hospitals and a home for people with mental retardation involved in the case were grossly understaffed and the programs of treatment and habilitation afforded the residents were extremely inadequate.

4. **PARC. Bowman et al. v. Commonwealth of Pennsylvania.** 334 F. Supp. 279 (1971). It was alleged that the retarded plaintiffs had been denied access to education and, furthermore, that the plaintiffs had been deprived of due process by the U.S. Constitution.

5. **Mills v. Board of Education of the District of Columbia.** 348 F. Supp. 866 (1972). A class action suit was filed in 1971 in the District of Columbia to compel the school board to provide appropriate education for students with mental retardation, physical handicaps, emotional disturbances, hyperactivity, and other handicaps.

6. **Stuart v. Napp.** 443 F. Supp. 1235 (D. Ct., 1978). Plaintiffs argued that expulsion of a learning disabled youth with a history of learning difficulties constituted a denial of the right to an appropriate education.

7. **S-1 v. Turlington.** no. 78–8020 (S.D. FL. 1979). Seven students with mental retardation alleged that their misconduct was the result of their handicap and that subsequent expulsion by the school was a denial of their right to an appropriate education.

8. **Board of Education v. Rowley.** 458 U.S. 176 (1982). Parents of a child with a profound hearing impairment filed suit alleging the school district's refusal to provide a sign language interpreter violated their daughter's right to a free, appropriate public education.

9. **Smith v. Robinson.** 104 C. St., 3457 (1984). Parents sought reimbursement of legal fees incurred during a lawsuit charging violation of their child's rights under PL 94-142.

10. **Irving Independent School District v. Tatro.** 104 S. Ct. 3371 (1984). Parents of a child born with spina bifida charged that clean intermittent catheterization was a supportive service necessary if their daughter was to benefit from special education.

11. **School District of Burlington, MA v. Department of Education of MA.** 105 S. Ct. 1996 (1985). The parents requested reimbursement for expenses incurred as the result of private school placement for their son who was learning disabled.

Legislation

1. **Public Law 88–164,** Mental Retardation Facilities and Community Mental Health Centers Act of 1963

2. **Public Law 89–10,** Elementary and Secondary Education Act of 1965—Title VI

3. **Public Law 91–230,** Elementary, Secondary, and Other Educational Amendments of 1969

4. **Public Law 93–380,** Title VI B—Education of the Handicapped Amendment (Mathias Amendment) of 1973

5. **Public Law 94–142,** Education for All Handicapped Children Act of 1975

6. **Public Law 98–410,** Education of Handicapped Act Amendment of 1983

7. **Public Law 99–955,** Rehabilitation Act Amendments of 1986

8. **Public Law 99–457,** Education of the Handicapped Act Amendments of 1986

9. **Public Law 99–172,** Handicapped Children's Protection Act of 1986

10. **Public Law 101–476,** Individuals with Disabilities Education Act (IDEA), 1990

APPENDIX B
Pennstar IEP Manager

Pennstar

IEP Manager
(Features of the IEP Software)

- PennStar creates an IEP that is saved to disk. It may be retrieved for editing and printing at any time. In subsequent years, an existing PennStar IEP Manager on disk may be revised by changing only the information that needs to be updated; delete objectives that have been achieved; modify objectives that need to be maintained; enter new objectives.

- A draft IEP may be prepared before the IEP conference. Changes can be made to the draft during the course of the meeting. A final IEP may be printed at the meeting and given to the parents before they go home.

- A complete curriculum is included that may be used with students of all developmental levels. Over 3 million unique objective statements may be generated with the delivered curriculum base.

- The curriculum may be edited to meet local needs. The TEACHER EDIT DISK permits the user to revise, delete, add to, or rearrange menu items on the Subject Area disks. The MASTER EDIT DISK provides for adding or deleting entire Subject Areas and Goal Areas. A complete locally developed curriculum may be loaded into the PennStar software. Each PennStar IEP Manager sold includes a TEACHER EDIT DISK. Only one MASTER EDIT DISK is provided per local education agency.

- Objectives written by itinerant or departmental teachers may be merged into a single IEP on one disk.

- Prior computer knowledge is not required.

- PennStar IEP Manager is menu-driven and very user-friendly. However, it is a powerful computer application and requires some study and practice to gain proficiency.

- A complete Objective Statement consisting of Objective Stem, up to three Conditions, Level of Achievement, Evaluation Schedule, and Method of Evaluation may be entered from pull-down menus with no typing. However, any of these menu items may be modified on the fly to express a particular student's specific educational needs.

- Changes made with the TEACHER EDIT DISK or the MASTER EDIT DISK are carried over into any Planned Courses produced with the edited version of the Subject Area disks.

Source: Adapted from Pennsylvania Department of Education, Bureau of Special Education. Special Education Resource System. September 1988.

APPENDIX C
Technical Competencies for Special Education Teachers, Self-Assessment

Technology Competencies for Special Education Teachers

Self-Assessment

A. Edward Blackhurst
Department of Special Education
University of Kentucky

DIRECTIONS: Provide an assessment of how well you can perform each of these tasks. Use the following key:

X = Not interested in this competency
C = Already competent in this area
I = Have some skills in this area; want to improve them
A = Interested in developing an awareness in this area
S = Want to develop skills in this area

NAME: _____ DATE: _____

In order to use technology effectively in special programs, teachers should be able to . . .

Acquire a body of knowledge about the use of microcomputers and related technology in special education.

1. Explain historical developments and trends in the application of microcomputers and related technology in special education.   X   C   I   A   S

2. Define terms and concepts related to technology applications in special education.   X   C   I   A   S

X = Not interested in this competency
C = Already competent in this area
I = Have some skills in this area; want to improve them
A = Interested in developing an awareness in this area
S = Want to develop skills in this area

3. Identify major issues associated with the use of technology in special education.   X C I A S

4. Identify ways that microcomputers and related technology, such as interactive video, robotics, and adaptive devices, can be incorporated into the special education curriculum to meet the instructional goals and objective of students.   X C I A S

5. Describe criteria for making decisions about the selection and purchase of microcomputers and related technology.   X C I A S

6. Read, evaluate, and apply information about technology applications in special education that appear in the professional literature and trade magazines.   X C I A S

7. Describe findings of research on technology use in special education.   X C I A S

8. Participate in activities of professional organizations that focus upon applications of technology in special education.   X C I A S

9. Maintain a professional development program to ensure the acquisition of knowledge and skills about new developments in technology as they become available.   X C I A S

Evaluate microcomputer software and related materials for their potential application in special education programs.

10. Identify the purpose of the instructional program, its objectives, and the validity of its content.   X C I A S

11. Determine the characteristics of learners for whom the program is appropriate.   X C I A S

12. Describe the format and ways information is presented to the learner.   X C I A S

13. Determine the extent of student control over the program.   X C I A S

14. Describe the commands required to use the materials, the academic and physical demands placed on the student, and the speed and accuracy of the program.   X C I A S

X = Not interested in this competency
C = Already competent in this area
I = Have some skills in this area; want to improve them
A = Interested in developing an awareness in this area
S = Want to develop skills in this area

15. Identify the type and frequency of feedback and reinforcement provided by the program.   X C I A S

16. Determine the extent of branching within the program.   X C I A S

17. Identify the options that exist to enable the teacher to modify features of the program.   X C I A S

18. Determine the adequacy of program documentation.   X C I A S

Develop a plan for technology use in a special education program.

19. Articulate goals and a philosophy for using technology in special education.   X C I A S

20. Identify elements of the special education curriculum for which technology applications are appropriate and ways they can be implemented.   X C I A S

21. Determine the physical requirements for implementing various technology systems in a special education classroom.   X C I A S

22. Ensure that special education students have equitable access to technology in any plans that are developed.   X C I A S

23. Prepare guidelines and rules for technology use in the special education classroom.   X C I A S

24. Identify resources available to support the use of technology in special education.   X C I A S

25. Develop a budget for technology applications in a special education classroom.   X C I A S

26. Identify funding sources for technology hardware, software, and accessories.   X C I A S

27. Write proposals to obtain funds for technology hardware and software.   X C I A S

Use technology in special education assessment and planning.

28. Identify programs that can be used for assessing exceptional children and planning their educational programs.   X C I A S

X = Not interested in this competency
C = Already competent in this area
I = Have some skills in this area; want to improve them
A = Interested in developing an awareness in this area
S = Want to develop skills in this area

---

29. Use microcomputers to administer tests to exceptional children.   X C I A S

30. Use software programs that can score and interpret the results of
standardized tests.   X C I A S

31. Use microcomputers to generate Assessment reports.   X C I A S

32. Use microcomputers to record observational data in special education
environments.   X C I A S

33. Use computer software programs to analyze, summarize, and report
student performance data to aid instructional decision making.   X C I A S

34. Use a microcomputer program to generate an Individualized Education
Program (IEP).   X C I A S

35. Explain the pros and cons of computerized programs that generate IEPs.   X C I A S

Use technology to facilitate instruction in special education programs.

36. Use technology to support effective instructional practices.   X C I A S

37. Arrange the physical environment to facilitate the use of technology.   X C I A S

38. Teach special education students to operate equipment and run
microcomputer software.   X C I A S

39. Teach students how to use microcomputers to increase their personal
productivity and independence.   X C I A S

40. Identify and use appropriate tutorial software programs.   X C I A S

41. Use drill and practice programs appropriately.   X C I A S

42. Incorporate simulation and problem solving programs into the
curriculum.   X C I A S

43. Use microcomputers to teach students written composition and
communication skills.   X C I A S

44. Teach students to use microcomputers for telecommunications and to
access electronic databases.   X C I A S

45. Use computers and related software for reinforcement.   X C I A S

X = Not interested in this competency
C = Already competent in this area
I = Have some skills in this area; want to improve them
A = Interested in developing an awareness in this area
S = Want to develop skills in this area

46. Use peripheral devices, such as printers, hand controllers, modems, and graphics tablets.   X C I A S

47. Evaluate the effectiveness of technology applications in the special education classroom.   X C I A S

48. Adhere to ethical standards when applying technology in special education.   X C I A S

Use technology to compensate for learning barriers that are due to communication disorders, physical disabilities, or visual impairments.

49. Determine the adaptive switches, software, and related equipment needed for students with communication disorders, physical disabilities, or visual impairments.   X C I A S

50. Connect and use alternate keyboards, other adaptive input and output devices, and construct materials for their use.   X C I A S

51. Construct adaptive switches to control access to computers.   X C I A S

52. Use technology to enable students to control other devices in their environment.   X C I A S

53. Use scanning devices and programs to facilitate single key and switch operation of computers.   X C I A S

54. Use a speech synthesizer and the software that controls it.   X C I A S

55. Use electronic communication boards and augmentative communication aids.   X C I A S

56. Use software and hardware that presents magnified text for partially sighted students.   X C I A S

Use the microcomputer to generate teaching aids for the special education classroom.

57. Use software programs to produce signs, transparency masters, and other visual aids.   X C I A S

58. Use software programs to produce worksheets for student use.   X C I A S

59. Design databases that students can use to store and retrieve information.   X C I A S

X = Not interested in this competency
C = Already competent in this area
I = Have some skills in this area; want to improve them
A = Interested in developing an awareness in this area
S = Want to develop skills in this area

---

60. Use instructional shell programs and authoring systems to develop computer-assisted instruction lessons. X C I A S

61. Use test generation software programs to develop test banks and prepare examinations. X C I A S

62. Use instructional data graphing and analysis programs. X C I A S

63. Use gradebook software programs to store and report student grades. X C I A S

Use a microcomputer as an aid to personal productivity.

64. Use a word processor to prepare lesson plans, class notes, correspondence, and other written documents. X C I A S

65. Use software utility programs, such as mail merging programs and spelling checkers. X C I A S

66. Use database programs to maintain student records and resource files. X C I A S

67. Use an electronic spreadsheet program to store and manipulate numerical data. X C I A S

68. Perform statistical analyses with microcomputer software. X C I A S

69. Use telecommunication systems and electronic message services (e.g., SpecialNet). X C I A S

70. Access information from electronic databases to support professional activities (e.g., ERIC). X C I A S

Disseminate information about applications of technology in special education.

71. Maintain a resource file of information about technology in special education. X C I A S

72. Provide consultation and technical assistance to colleagues and to handicapped individuals about the use of technology. X C I A S

73. Serve as a resource to parents of exceptional children who have microcomputers and related equipment available for use at home. X C I A S

74. Make presentations about technology use in special education to lay and professional groups. X C I A S

X = Not interested in this competency
C = Already competent in this area
I = Have some skills in this area; want to improve them
A = Interested in developing an awareness in this area
S = Want to develop skills in this area

75. Conduct in-service training on technology applications in special education.   X C I A S

76. Prepare articles and reports about technology use in special education.   X C I A S

Assemble, operate, and maintain the components of technology systems in a special education environment.

77. Connect audio and video equipment and input and output devices such as disk drives, printers, monitors, speech synthesizers, graphics tablets, video systems, and modems.   X C I A S

78. Configure software to ensure that all of its features will work properly with the equipment being used.   X C I A S

79. Explain operations that could cause hardware damage if not performed in an appropriate manner.   X C I A S

80. State the environmental conditions under which various technologies operate most efficiently.   X C I A S

81. Demonstrate the proper care of microcomputer disks and describe the effects that dust, magnetic fields, temperature, liquids, and physical abuse can have on them.   X C I A S

82. Use simple diagnostics to determine problems that may exist when a piece of equipment or software program fails to operate properly.   X C I A S

83. Perform routine maintenance of a technology system.   X C I A S

Use microcomputer operating system commands.

84. Initialize diskettes in preparation for using them to store information for various applications.   X C I A S

85. Make backup copies of commercial software and copies of public domain software using programs that will copy entire disks and programs that will copy one file at a time.   X C I A S

86. Use the operating system and utility software programs that accompany the computer being used.   X C I A S

87. Type and run computer programs that are printed in computer magazines.   X C I A S

APPENDIX D
Computer Basics

Many persons who choose to work in the area of instruction will have a good background in the basic terminology of computers and computing. Others will have a less extensive background. Still others will be entirely new to the area. This appendix is devoted to providing basic terminology and concepts in lay educators' language. If these items are familiar to you, you can refresh your memory or move to another section of the text. Better yet, help a fellow student master this basic, but required material so that each of you may be a better facilitator of the learning of the child with special needs. (See Figure 3-5 on one way you might introduce computer use into your classroom when you become a teacher.)

The Computer

The computer is defined as: "a device capable of solving problems or manipulating data by accepting data, performing prescribed operations (mathematical or logical) on the data and supplying the results of these operations" (Spencer, *Computer Dictionary*, p. 36).

A computer system is what most people really mean when they talk about a computer. This system consists of a basic computer (CPU), some sort of input device such as a keyboard that allows the user to enter information, and some sort of output device such as a video screen or printer that provides results to the user. In all instances, whether built into the machine or plugged into the computer, all systems have some type of memory and, generally, some storage facility. While not technically correct, memory and storage are often used as synonyms. Precisely, memory pertains to the part of storage where instructions to the computer are executed, while storage is a unit (or thing) where text or data can be entered (e.g., a disk can be used for storage).

DEFINITION: Hardware

Physical equipment such as CPU, memory, input/output (I/O) devices, and connections that form a computer system.

DEFINITION: Software

A set of programs, procedures, routines, and documents associated with the operation of a computer system. Software is the name given to the programs that cause a computer to carry out particular operations.

DEFINITION: Assistive Device

A mechanical or electronic unit that facilitates the use of a computer for a student with a disability.

A computer system consists of the following:

Input Device: A unit used to get data into the CPU from the user (card reader, keyboard, acoustic character recognition unit, light pen, etc.)

Output Device: A unit used for taking data out of a computer and presenting them in the desired form to the user (printer, video screen, braille card, etc.)

Arithmetic-Logic Unit: The portion of the CPU in which arithmetic and logic operations (e.g., determining numerical order) are performed.

Control Unit Section: That portion of the CPU that directs the step-by-step operation of the entire system.

Storage Device: A device or medium that can accept data or instructions, hold these, and deliver them on demand at a later time. (primary and auxiliary storage are features of most systems.)

The CPU generally contains the primary memory unit, the arithmetic/logic unit, and the control units. Incidentally, no piece of a computer system is of much use without the other elements (e.g., without a video screen, it is impossible to view the results of computation).

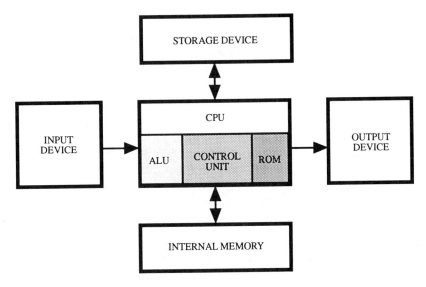

Figure D-1
Hardware components
of a computer system.

Although the term *computer* means a number of things to a number of people, computers in their most basic form are electronic devices that perform computation, including both arithmetic and logic operations, without the intervention of a human being. Again, much of what a computer does is rather simple; it just does it so fast and with such accuracy that humans have transferred this role to the computer. The use of a computer as support for instruction is more a function of the interaction of hardware (discussed above) and software (to be discussed next) rather than the actual "number crunching" capabilities of the computer. Regardless of the results of computer processing—the really showy results of computer applications—the computer performs these major operations:

1. Arithmetic—addition, subtraction, multiplication, and division of data
2. Logic—comparison of the magnitude of one number with another number to determine order (i.e., $<$, $=$, $>$)
3. Input/Output—receiving data for storage and/or processing or causing data to be provided back to a user

The word *data* here refers to items ranging from student test scores to text material stating activities to be included in the IEP. Data can be entered, "acted on," and returned to the user; it can be entered, stored, modified, changed, and then returned to the user; or it can be entered, used, refined, expanded, and become a database for individual decisions (i.e., IEP decisions) or group activities (i.e., reports to federal funding agencies). "Data" is a word that often is equated with numbers; for many applications, however, data are text, graphs, charts, music, or pictures.

Location of these "data" is in what we call memory or storage. The magnitude of this is usually measured in terms of K (2 to the 10th power, or 1,024 in decimal notation). For example, a machine is said to have 256K of storage, which is equal to 256,000 bits of information. The terms *storage* and *memory* are often used synonymously. Technically, memory is the part of storage in which instructions are executed. Memory excludes auxiliary storage devices such as a disk, diskette, and magnetic tape.

Computers use a binary number system of zeros and ones to process input/words or numbers. These are called bits (binary digits). Numbers (0–9), letters (A–Z), and special characters (*, ", /, etc.) are converted to a series of bits (0s and 1s). These generally are used in combinations of 8. For example, the letter "A" is stored in memory as 01000001. Notice there are 8 spaces. The letter "Z" is stored in memory as 01011010. Each of these 8 spaces represents one byte. One byte is equal to 8 bits. Bytes are used to describe the amount of memory (RAM) or (ROM) a computer has. For example, 64K means a microcomputer has 65536 bytes of RAM. (K comes from the word *kilobyte*; each kilobyte equals 1024 bytes.)

DEFINITION: Read Only Memory (ROM)

Permanently programmed memory with one set of frequently used instructions. The memory is not erased when the machine is turned off, but the memory cannot be changed by the user.

DEFINITION: Ramdon Access Memory (RAM)

A memory from which a user calls up data or enters information and instructions. This is the "working" area of the computer.

Software

The list of instructions that is provided to the computer, whether written by the user or preloaded from a vendor, constitutes what are called programs. Software is generally a broader term, which includes programs, procedures, rules, and associated documentation. Various types or classes of software are used, and include system software, application software, and integrated software.

Applications software is the collection of items most known to the general user—word-processing packages, instructional programs, and games. Systems software—generally not the concern of end users—is that set of software that is a part of or made available with the computer system and determines how application software (programs) are run. Integrated software allows the use of two or more applications concurrently. For example, a user could be word processing while at the same time the machine is performing calculations for use in a spreadsheet.

When a programmer develops a software package and adds a teacher's manual, a set of test questions, workbooks, slides, a tutorial disk, and so forth, the resulting package in often called courseware.

Summary

This appendix was provided for readers who may not be familiar with computer terminology. When people make reference to a computer they usually mean a CPU, an input device (e.g., a keyboard), and an output device (e.g., a video screen and/or printer). Built into the CPU is usually some sort of storage device that accepts instructions and can hold them in memory. Computers are useful classroom tools because their speed and accuracy interact with software in such a way that the machine can support teaching and learning and/or make the environment for a person with a disability more accessible.

The term *software* includes programs, procedures, rules, and associated documentation. Types of software include system, application, and integrated software. Courseware is a software package that includes a teacher's manual, test questions, tutorial disk, and so forth.

APPENDIX E
Key Times/Events for Computer and Special Needs Learner

KEY TIMES/EVENTS IN THE EVOLUTION OF COMPUTERS AND COMPUTING	DATES	KEY TIMES/EVENTS IN SERVICES TO SPECIAL NEEDS STUDENTS
Pascal invents one of the first adding machines using cogged wheels for storage and processing of information.	1640–1650	
	1775	Birthdate of French physician Jean-Marie Gaspard Itard, known for his work with Victor the "wild boy of Aveyron."
	1785	Birthdate of Louis Laurent Marie Clerc, a pioneer in deaf education in the United States.
	1787	Birthdate of Thomas Hopkins Gallaudet, American teacher who established the first school for the deaf in the United States in 1817.
Jacquard develops the automatic textile loom using punched cards.	1790–1800	
	1802	Birthdate of Dorothea Lynde Dix, American social reformer.
	1809	Birthdate of Louis Braille, developer of braille code for the blind.
Charles Babbage proposes a computer capable of all functions except control—the difference engine. He later proposes, but does not develop, the analytic engine, which is the first general purpose computer.	1812–1850	

(continued)

Appendix E (continued)

KEY TIMES/EVENTS IN THE EVOLUTION OF COMPUTERS AND COMPUTING	DATES	KEY TIMES/EVENTS IN SERVICES TO SPECIAL NEEDS STUDENTS
Augusta Ada Byron, daughter of Lord Byron (the first programmer), begins working with Charles Babbage.	1842	
	1857	Birthdate of Alfred Binet, codeveloper of the Simon–Binet Test, with Theodore Simon.
	1859	Birthdate of John Dewey, American psychologist, philosopher, and educational reformer.
	1864	Gallaudet College celebrates its inauguration and begins to recruit deaf pupils.
	1865	Birthdate of Charles Horace Mayo, cofounder of the Mayo Clinic.
	1866	Birthdate of Annie Sullivan, teacher of Helen Keller.
	1876	First meeting of the American Association on Mental Retardation (AAMR).
	1877	Birthdate of Lewis Madison Terman, publisher of the Stanford Binet—the first important intelligence test in the United States.
	1879	Birthdate of Samuel Torry Orton, pioneer in the diagnosis and treatment of dyslexia.
Census Bureau hires Herman Hollerith to develop procedures and machine to speed up processing of 1880 census data.	1880–1893	
	1895	The Helen Keller National Center for Deaf-Blind Youths and Adults is founded.
Herman Hollerith leaves the Census Bureau and founds the Hollerith Tabulating Machine Company (the forerunner of IBM).	1896	Birthdate of psychologist David Wechsler, in Lespedi, Romania.

(continued)

Appendix E (*continued*)

KEY TIMES/EVENTS IN THE EVOLUTION OF COMPUTERS AND COMPUTING	DATES	KEY TIMES/EVENTS IN SERVICES TO SPECIAL NEEDS STUDENTS
	1903	Birthdate of Benjamin Spock, pediatrician.
James Powers develops other machines for processing census data using some of Hollerith's ideas. Over time his company becomes Sperry Rand and still later, Unisys.	1910	
	1914	Birthdate of Dr. Jonas Salk, developer of the Salk vaccine for polio.
	1922	Birthdate of Eunice Shriver, founder of the Special Olympics.
	1922	Charter date for the Council for Exceptional Children (CEC).
Thomas Watson becomes president of CTR and changes its name to IBM.	1924	
	1925	The American Speech-Language-Hearing Association is organized.
	1940	The National Federation of the Blind is founded in Wilkes Barre, Pennsylvania.
MARK I is developed by John Atanasoff at Harvard ENIAC—first actual electronic computer.	1944	
	1946	Charter date for the American Association for Gifted Children (AAGC), the oldest organization for gifted children in the United States.
Census Bureau accepts delivery of UNIVAC I from Remington Rand. First Ferranti Mark I is delivered to the University of Manchester in England. IBM decides to produce the 701, the first electronic binary computer.	1951	
IBM announces the 650, the first mass-produced computer, and sets to work on the 704.	1954	*Brown v. Topeka Board of Education* (347 #U.S. 483) Polio vaccinations are given in the Pittsburgh school system.

(continued)

Appendix E (*continued*)

KEY TIMES/EVENTS IN THE EVOLUTION OF COMPUTERS AND COMPUTING	DATES	KEY TIMES/EVENTS IN SERVICES TO SPECIAL NEEDS STUDENTS
First FORTRAN compiler goes to work with an IBM 704.	1957	CEC charter date of the Division for the Visually Handicapped (DVH) and the Teacher Education Division (TED).
IBM announces its popular 1401 computer.	1959	
ASCII becomes a standard. Integrated circuit is developed.	1963	The Council for Children with Behavioral Disorders (CCBD) is formally affiliated with CEC. Dr. Sam Kirk coins the term *learning disability*. President John F. Kennedy calls for "a national program to combat mental retardation." The CEC Division on Mental Retardation is organized.
IBM gives birth to its unified System/360 family.	1964	The Division on Mental Retardation (CECMR) is formally affiliated with the CEC.
Digital Equipment unveils the PDP-8, pioneering the minicomputer path.	1965	President Lyndon B. Johnson signs the National Technical Institute for the Deaf Act into law.
	1966	Executive Order 11280, signed by President Lyndon B. Johnson, establishes the president's Committee on Mental Retardation.
	1967	The Division on Children with Communication Disorders, an affiliate of the CEC, receives its charter.
Memory and microprocessor maker Intel Corp. is formed. The first software patent (for a sort) is issued to Martin Goetz.	1968	The date of enactment of PL 90-247, the Elementary & Secondary Education Amendments of 1967. The first Special Olympic Games are held in Chicago.
IBM lives up to its 1968 pledge to "unbundle" software.	1969	

(*continued*)

Appendix E (*continued*)

KEY TIMES/EVENTS IN THE EVOLUTION OF COMPUTERS AND COMPUTING	DATES	KEY TIMES/EVENTS IN SERVICES TO SPECIAL NEEDS STUDENTS
Amdahl Corp. is formed, kicking off plug-compatible mainframe movement.	1970	Enactment of PL 91-205, legislation to insure that certain federally constructed facilities be accessible to people with physical handicaps.
The microprocessor, invented by Ted Hoff, goes to market as the Intel 4004.	1971	
Supercomputer designer Seymour Cray founds his own firm.	1972	
	1973	The Division for Early Childhood becomes formally affiliated with CEC.
Privacy Act	1974	The Council
Wang delivers word-processing products that lead the wave of WP wares.	1975	President Gerald Ford signs PL 94-142, the Education for All Handicapped Children Act.
AT&T offers Dataphone switched digital service. Microsoft and Apple Computer are formed; the Apple I is introduced. Hobby Computer Market booms with Altair 8800, Radio Shack TRS-80 PC, and Commodore's PET PC.	1976	
	1977	The First International Winter Special Olympics Games are held in Steamboat Springs, Colorado, January 5–11.
	1978	Charter date for the National Center for Learning Disabilities.
	1979	The Accrediation Council on Services for People with Developmental Disabilities (ACDD) is founded.
IBM announces its personal computer with MS-DOS developed by Microsoft.	1981	
Lotus Development Corp. sets up shop and announces Lotus 1-2-3 spreadsheet software.	1982	
Apple brings Macintosh PC to market.	1984	

(*continued*)

Appendix E (*continued*)

KEY TIMES/EVENTS IN THE EVOLUTION OF COMPUTERS AND COMPUTING	DATES	KEY TIMES/EVENTS IN SERVICES TO SPECIAL NEEDS STUDENTS
	1986	The Division for Learning Disabilities (DLD) is chartered as a division of CEC.
IBM announces its PS/2 family, and rival AT&T debuts its PC from Olivetti.	1986	
Concentrating on its core computer business, IBM spins off low-end printer, keyboard, and typewriter operations. IBM introduces the System/390 family.	1990	The Division for Culturally and Linguistically Diverse Exceptional Learners and the Division of International Special Education and Services are formally affiliated with CEC. Charter date for the CEC Division for Research. President George Bush signs the Americans with Disabilities Act (ADA) into law.
	1993	71st CEC Convention is held in San Antonio, Texas.

APPENDIX F
Programming Languages

Communication with computers is done through programs. Most computer users take for granted that the program is in place and will do what it is supposed to do. Generally the user needs to know little (or nothing) about programming to use a program or package. If you are curious, however, below is a brief explanation of programming languages.

The term *computer program* as used here is a sequence of instructions permitting a computer to achieve a particular task. These programs are written in a language that is a set of codes, representations, and conventions used to transfer information in terms of instructions to the computer.

Power and Ease

A note about the power and ease of any computer language is in order. The power of a language is measured in its efficiency in solving varied and complex problems. General agreement as to features of such "power" include:

Vocabulary: the number of commands (e.g., add "A" to "B"), functions (e.g., squaring a number), and descriptors (e.g., a word that indexes information) available to the user

Variable Types: how many types of data (e.g., a representation of information, a number, letter, etc.) the language can accommodate

Functions: the number, complexity of commands that can be defined with one-word terms (e.g., End, Return)

Arrays: a series of related items

Matrices:	a group of elements (numbers, symbols, or characters) organized as a rectangular grid and located as a unit. Each element can be referenced by a position on the grid (e.g., row 1, column 3)

The "ease of use" features include:

Syntax:	the required order of terms and punctuation in any line of code
Format:	indentation, line number, and rigid nature of layout
Variable Names:	user-assigned, but limitations of length affect clarity (e.g., how many letters one is restricted to in naming a file)
Editor:	a built-in editor is a major help to the programmer
Portability:	permits running the same program on different computers
Structure:	may be restrictive, but insures logical thinking

Flowcharting

When the concept of a stored program was introduced in the late 1940s the programmers responsible for translating the ideas of how to solve a problem or perform a function needed a means of expressing the logic of what they were doing. This expression often took the form of a flowchart. This precise sequence of graphic representations of the program's logic became sufficiently important to require a standard set of symbols to represent the ideas. For example,

Figure F-1
Standard symbols on a
flowchart.

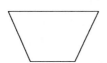

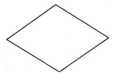

INPUT/OUTPUT

Any funtion of an imput/out device (making information available for processing, recording processing information, tape positioning, etc.).

DECISION

The decision function is used to document points in the program where a branch to alternate paths is possible based upon variable conditions.

Finally, the logic of a simple program follows:

Figure F-2
Example of a flowchart
for a simple program.

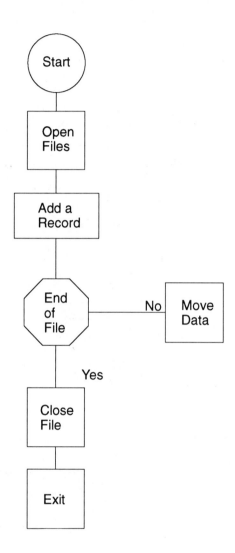

Machine Languages

The earliest computers could be programmed only by experts using binary codes unique to each computer. This type of programming involves the difficult task of translating instructions into strings of ones and zeros. Since the binary machine code for each type of computer is unique, programmers using the machine's language must have detailed knowledge of the internal workings of the specific CPU. To accomplish even the simplest of tasks, the programmer writes a long series of detailed instructions, specifying machine language addresses for every instruction as well as for every data item used. Additional instructions are included for every switch and indicator used in the program. The resulting program consists of columns of binary numbers, difficult to decipher and extremely error-prone. In addition, if the programmer wants a different computer to perform the same task, the program has to be completely rewritten using the machine code peculiar to the new computer.

DEFINITION: Machine Language

A language that can be used directly by a computer without intermediate processing.

Assembler Languages

Rather than forcing the programmer to write in the binary code native to the computer, assembler language allows the use of convenient alphabetic abbreviations called mnemonics to represent operation codes and abstract symbols to represent operands (memory addresses and data items). The resulting program is more intelligible and less error-prone. Since the program is no longer written in ones and zeros, the computer cannot directly understand it. Assembler language makes programming easier for humans, but one step harder for computers. In order for the computer to execute a series of assembler language instructions, a program called an assembler must first be used. The assembler allows the computer to translate a program written in an assembler language into machine language instructions it can understand. Only after the translation has occurred can the computer execute the programmer's commands.

Despite the relative ease of assembler language programming, it is still a machine- rather than human-oriented process. Assembler language instructions correspond in a one-on-one relationship with their machine language equivalents for the particular computer being used. Thus, each assembler language is specific to the instruction set of one computer. For this reason, assembler language programming is widely used by systems programmers (persons who write operating systems, etc.) since it provides them with greater control and flexibility in designing a system for a particular computer. For most other programs, another step toward human programmer ease and convenience is needed.

> ## DEFINITION: Assembler Language
>
> A programming language whose instructions are usually in one-to-one correspondence with machine instructions and may provide other facilities such as microinstructions.

Procedure-Oriented Languages

These are the first programming languages that are human rather than machine-oriented. Instructions in these languages are called statements and resemble a cross between human language and standard mathematical notation. Each individual high-level language statement generates several machine instructions when translated into machine language by language translator programs called compilers or interpreters.

> ## DEFINITION: Procedure-Oriented Language
>
> A problem-oriented language that facilitates the expression of a procedure as an explicit algorithm, for example, *FORTRAN, ALGOL, COBOL, PL/1.*

Problem-Oriented Languages

These actually encompass several distinct categories of programming language, each of which aims at simplifying the task of imparting instructions to a computer. Some of these include natural languages, application generators, query languages, report writers, and data manipulation languages. They are called fourth-generation languages to differentiate them from the three earlier categories: machine language (first generation); assembler language (second generation); and procedure-oriented language (third generation).

> ## DEFINITION: Object-Oriented Programming
>
> An approach that enables the building of programs from modular units that have attributes transferable from one program to another.

A major area of research and experimentation in the computer field is the development of nonprocedural natural languages. These programming tools are extremely human-oriented in that they free the programmer from writing detailed procedures telling the computer how to complete a given task. Using statements very close to English or other human languages, the programmer simply specifies the desired results. The compiler and the computer do the rest. Communication with a computer using natural language is as easy as ordinary conversation in one's natural language. New syntax and special meanings are eliminated, making error-free programs much easier to achieve. Programs called intelligent compilers are being developed to translate natural language programs into structured machine-coded instructions that can be executed by computers.

DEFINITION: Problem-Oriented Language

A programming language that is especially suitable for a given class of problems.

Many persons see a fifth type of language as the language that uses artificial intelligence techniques to achieve user goals.

APPENDIX G
Educational Software
Evaluation Form

Educational Software Evaluation Form

Program Title: _____ Subject Area: _____

Publisher: _____ Cost: _____ Copyright: _____

Disk Size: 3.5 _____ 5.25 _____ Required Hardware: _____

I. PROGRAM CHARACTERISTICS
   1. Instructional range:
      grade levels _____ ability levels _____

   2. Instructional grouping for use:

      individual _____ small group (size: _____) large group (size: _____)

   3. Execution time _____

   4. Prerequisite skills needed? _____

   5. Nature of program
      _____ A. Drill and practice   _____ F. Testing
      _____ B. Tutorial   _____ G. Instructional management
      _____ C. Gaming   _____ H. Tool
      _____ D. Stimulation   _____ I. Problem solving
      _____ E. Dialog   _____ J. Other: _____

   6. Objectives are clearly stated: _____ Yes _____ No

II. DESCRIPTION OF PROGRAM:

....

....

....

III. CONTENT

	low			high
The content of the program is accurate.	·	·	·	·
The content is appropriate for the objectives.	·	·	·	·
Program is compatible with other materials.	·	·	·	·
The level of sophistication is appropriate.	·	·	·	·
The content is free of bias.	·	·	·	·

IV. RUNNING THE PROGRAM

Instructions are clear and easy to understand.	Yes	?	No	N/A
Screen display is well designed.	Yes	?	No	N/A
Program is free from bugs.	Yes	?	No	N/A
Material is well organized & presented effectively.	Yes	?	No	N/A
Branching is provided.	Yes	?	No	N/A
Graphics and sound are used as enhancement not embellishment.	Yes	?	No	N/A
Student involvement is active.	Yes	?	No	N/A
Feedback both negative and positive is effective and not demeaning.	Yes	?	No	N/A
Cues and prompts are clear.	Yes	?	No	N/A
Pacing and sequencing can be controlled.	Yes	?	No	N/A
Instructions can be skipped if desired.	Yes	?	No	N/A
Instructions and help screens can be accessed at any time.	Yes	?	No	N/A
A tutorial is provided.	Yes	?	No	N/A
Program will tolerate inappropriate input without crashing.	Yes	?	No	N/A
Program achieves the stated objectives.	Yes	?	No	N/A

V. SOCIAL CHARACTERISTICS

	Present/Negative	Present/Positive	Not
Present	_____	_____	_____
Competition	_____	_____	_____
Cooperation	_____	_____	_____
Moral issues/Value judgments	_____	_____	_____
Summary of student performance	_____	_____	_____

VI. STRENGTHS AND WEAKNESSES

Identify the major strengths:

Identify the major weaknesses:

VII. DOCUMENTATION

1. Is documentation provided?   Yes   No
2. Is it well organized for ease of use?   Yes   No
3. Is it understandable?   Yes   No

VIII. RECOMMENDATION

_____ Excellent program; would recommend purchase
_____ Good program; consider purchase
_____ Fair program; wait
_____ Poor program; would not purchase
_____ Other Recommendations:

IX. REVIEW

A published review of the program was located.   Yes   No
   If yes, identify location:

X. AWARDS

Identify any awards won:

APPENDIX H
1987 Statement on Software Copyright

1987 Statement on Software Copyright

An ICCE* Policy Statement

Right to reprint granted by the ICCE Software Copyright Committee.

Model District Policy on Software Copyright

It is the intent of [district] to adhere to the provisions of copyright laws in the area of microcomputer software. It is also the intent of the district to comply with the license agreements and/or policy statements contained in the software packages used in the district. In circumstances where the interpretation of the copyright law is ambiguous, the district shall look to the applicable license agreement to determine appropriate use of the software [or the district will abide by the approved Software Use Guidelines].

We recognize that computer software piracy is a major problem for the industry and that violations of copyright laws contribute to higher costs and greater efforts to prevent copying and/or lessen incentives for the development of effective educational uses of microcomputers. Therefore, in an effort to discourage violation of copyright laws and to prevent such illegal activities:

1. The ethical and practical implications of software piracy will be taught to educators and school children in all schools in the district (e.g., covered in fifth grade social studies classes).

2. District employees will be informed that they are expected to adhere to section 117 of the 1976 Copyright Act as amended in 1980, governing the use of software (e.g., each building principal will devote one faculty meeting to the subject each year).

*International Council for Computers in Education

3. When permission is obtained from the copyright holder to use software on a disk-sharing system, efforts will be made to secure this software from copying.

4. Under no circumstances shall illegal copies of copyrighted software be made or used on school equipment.

5. [Name or job title] of this school district is designated as the only individual who may sign license agreements for software for schools in the district. Each school using licensed software should have a signed copy of the software agreement.

APPENDIX I
Instructional Materials and Equipment

ACHIEVEMENT PRODUCTS

P.O. Box 547

Mineola, New York 11501

Large and small equipment, including items for positioning, adaptive feeding tools, and sound production devices, designed for early intervention programs.

AMERICAN ELECTROMEDICS CORP.

13 Sagamore Park Road

Hudson, New Hampshire 03051

Supply house for the *tympanometer*, an instrument for the identification, detection, and management of middle ear disease.

AMERICAN GUIDANCE SERVICE (AGS)

4201 Woodland Road

Circle Pines, Minnesota 55014

Instructional language, social and cognitive programs, and materials for skills development in young children.

ARISTA CORPORATION

2440 Eastand Way

P.O. Box 6146

Concord, California 94524

Comprehensive multisensory prereading and prearithmetic skills building programs with supporting audiovisual and concrete teaching devices.

ASIEP EDUCATIONAL COMPANY

3216 N.E. 27th

Portland, Oregon 97212

Assessment and instructional materials as well as consultation services for programs serving children with autism.

BARNELL LOFT, LTD.
958 Church Street
Baldwin, New York 11510
Workbooks designed to develop visual readiness for reading.

A. G. BELL PUBLICATIONS
3417 Volta Place, N.W.
Washington, D.C. 20007
Instructional audiovisual materials emphasizing the auditory-oral components of communication.

BEMISS–JASON CORPORATION
37600 Central Court
Newark, California 94560
Creative paper products and related craft materials for preschool handicapped or gifted children.

BENEFIC PRESS
1250 Sixth Avenue
San Diego, California 92101
Materials to develop thinking skills in children working at K–3 levels.

BFA EDUCATIONAL MEDIA
CBS Educational & Professional Pub.
2211 Michigan Avenue
Santa Monica, California 90404
Film and reading readiness materials for kindergarten and primary grades.

BORG–WARNER EDUCATIONAL SYSTEMS
600 West University Drive
Arlington Heights, Illinois 60004
System 80, individualized learning system for developing language skills and learning letter sounds.

BOWMAR/NOBLE PUBLISHERS, INC.
4563 Colorado Boulevard
Los Angeles, California 90039
Featured for this population is *Try: Experiences for Young Children* and other creative educational materials.

BRAULT & BOUTHILLER, LTD.
700 Beaumont
Montreal, Quebec, Canada H3N 1V5
Coordination games, puppets, puzzles, construction materials, and manipulatives for young children; prices in Canadian dollars.

C. C. PUBLICATIONS, INC.
P.O. Box 23699
Tigard, Oregon 97223

Materials include (1) screening test for apraxis; (2) fluency training for young children; and (3) cleft palate curriculum program.

CHILDCRAFT EDUCATION CORP.
20 Kilmer Road
Edison, New Jersey 08817

The "Growing Years" catalog includes furniture, equipment for physical development, blocks, puzzles, and other manipulatives, posters, and media equipment.

CLEARVUE, INC.
6666 N. Oliphant Avenue
Chicago, Illinois 60631

Of particular interest are the Alpha-Sound Program (foundations for reading through phonics) and The Basic Concepts Programs (shapes, colors, time, relationships, alphabet, numbers, social relationships, money, self-sufficiency, and survival).

COMMUNICATION SKILL BUILDERS
3130 N. Dodge Boulevard
P.O. Box 42050-K
Tucson, Arizona 85733

Variety of games and other activities for speech and language development.

COMMUNITY PLAYTHINGS
Rte. 213
Rifton, New York 12471

Specialized equipment for play, motor development, and the needs of physically handicapped preschoolers.

CONSTRUCTIVE PLAYTHINGS
11100 Harry Hines Boulevard
Dallas, Texas 75229

Curriculum materials, supplies, and equipment for infant and preschool education.

CONSULTING PSYCHOLOGISTS PRESS, INC.
P.O. Box 10096
Palo Alto, California 94303

Publishers of psychological tests and educational materials serving customers in the helping professions.

CROFT, INC.
4601 York Road
Baltimore Maryland 21212
Reading readiness materials with assessment component and teacher's guide.

CUISENAIRE CO. OF AMERICA, INC.
12 Church Street, Box D
New Rochelle, New York 10805
Manipulatives for comprehensive early math experiences.

CURRICULUM ASSOCIATES, INC.
5 Esquire Road
North Billerica, Massachusetts 01862
Publisher of many materials for basic skills development in the primary grades.
Also publisher of Brigance Inventory of Early Development.

DEVELOPMENTAL LEARNING MATERIALS
P.O. Box 4000
One DLM Park
Allen, Texas 75002

Classroom-tested and easy to use teaching aids for skill development in speech/
language, listening, and preacademic skills.

DISNEY SCHOOLHOUSE
350 South Buena Vista Street
Burbank, California 91521

Duplicating books for skills development, K–3. Includes a phonics program, language arts, math, social studies, health and safety, holidays, and back to school.
Also bulletin board kits.

D. JAY PRODUCTS, INC.
P.O. Box 797
Newark, New Jersey 07101
Colorfast and flame-resistant chenille and related products for crafts.

DORMAC, INC.
P.O. Box 752
Beaverton, Oregon 97075

Materials for clinical and home training for hearing impaired infants, 0–4 years.
Also precise language curriculum for the deaf multihandicapped.

EBSCO CURRICULUM MATERIALS
Div. EBSCO Industries, Inc.
Box 486
Birmingham, Alabama 35201
Materials for self-help and communication skills development. Suppliers of complete line of *Blissymbolics.*

EARMARK, INC.
1125 Dixwell Avenue
Hamden, Connecticut 06514
Auditory learning equipment for the smallest of preschoolers and older children who are hearing impaired.

THE ECONOMY COMPANY
P.O. Box 25308
1901 North Walnut Street
Oklahoma City, Oklahoma 73125
Materials for kindergarten including Crossties, comprehensive programming.

EDMARK CORP.
14350 N.E. 21st Street
Bellevue, Washington 98007
Printed and packaged instructional materials for use with young children and for professional development.

EDUCAT PUBLISHERS, INC.
P.O. Box 2891
Clinton, Iowa 52735
Separate catalog of special education instructional materials, multimedia programs, and assessment instruments.

EDUCATIONAL ACTIVITIES, INC.
1937 Grand Avenue
Baldwin, New York 11510
Multimedia programs at all levels including special education for preschool age children. Also records for teaching basic skills through music.

EDUCATIONAL MEDIA, INC.
3191 Westover Drive, SE
Washington, D.C. 20020
Creative wooden play structures to provide physical and mental stimulation in young children.

EDUCATIONAL PERFORMANCE ASSOCIATES
600 Broad Avenue
Ridgefield, New Jersey 07657

MISTER ROGERS and language development materials intended to aid teachers who work with preschool and primary grade handicapped or nonhandicapped children.

EDUCATIONAL TEACHING AIDS
159 West Kinzie Street
Chicago, Illinois 60610

Features *Chicago Early*, an assessment, prescriptive, and remediation instrument and manipulative kits, correlated to the instructional activities.

EDUCATORS PUBLISHING SERVICES, INC.
75 Moulton Street
Cambridge, Massachusetts 02238

Publishers of assessment instruments for identifying young children with communication problems, a questionnaire for parents, and games for early learning experiences.

ENVIRONMENTS, INC.
Beaufort Industrial Park
P.O. Box 1348
Beaufort, South Carolina 29902

Comprehensive variety of special education instructional materials for young children and professional literature for their teachers.

FILMAKERS LIBRARY, INC.
133 East 58th Street
Suite 703A
New York, New York 10022

Catalog of award-winning films concerned with handicapping conditions, child development, and language acquisition.

FLAGHOUSE, INC.
150 N. MacQuesten Pkwy.
Mount Vernon, New York 10550

Over 2,000 products, large and small equipment, designed to stimulate motor activity for balance, mobility, manipulation, socialization, and recreation.

FOLKWAYS RECORDS
43 W. 61st
New York, New York 10023

Records for developing basic skills and concepts in young children.

GAMCO INDUSTRIES, INC.
Box 1911
Big Spring, Texas 79720
Multimedia materials for basic skills development. Catalog provides content analysis for all products.

GOULD ATHLETIC SUPPLY CO.
3156 North 96 Street
Milwaukee, Wisconsin 53222
Equipment for physical education, adaptive physical education, therapeutic recreation, and special education skill building.

GREAT IDEAS, INC.
8005 Sacramento Street
Fair Oaks, California 95628
Manipulatives and lesson plans for teaching number concepts in kindergarten and first grade.

J. L. HAMMETT EDUCATIONAL SUPPLIES AND EQUIPMENT
P.O. Box 9057
Braintree, Massachusetts 02184
Large and small equipment for the instructional activities of young children.

THE HIGH/SCOPE PRESS
600 North River Street
Ypsilanti, Michigan 48197
Publishers of materials developed to provide practical alternatives to traditional ways of educating children, training teachers, and working with parents.

HIGHLIGHTS FOR CHILDREN
2300 West Fifth Avenue
P.O. Box 269
Columbus, Ohio 43272
Publishers of an educational magazine and other publications designed for children ages 2–12 years old.

HUBBARD
P.O. Box 104
Northbrook, Illinois 60062
Personal Care Programs are teaching strategies for use with moderately to severely mentally handicapped children.

HUMAN DEVELOPMENT TRAINING INSTITUTE
1727 Fifth Avenue
San Diego, California 92101
Materials for affective development of primary age children and for professional training.

HUMAN SCIENCES PRESS
72 Fifth Avenue
New York, New York 10011
Professional literature for training paraprofessionals to function in home-based programs.

IMPERIAL INTERNATIONAL LEARNING
P.O. Box 548
Kankakee, Illinois 60901
Instructional materials for basic readiness skills in reading.

INCENTIVES FOR LEARNING, INC.
600 West Van Buren Street
Chicago, Illinois 60607
Assessment and instructional materials for the development of language and motor skills in young children.

INNOVATIVE EDUCATIONAL MATERIALS
314 Upper Mountain Avenue
Upper Montclair, New Jersey 07043
Publishers of a criterion-referenced culture-fair assessment instrument used with children ages 3–16 to determine adaptive coping ability and an early identification screening instrument.

INTERMARK CORPORATION
24 Wilson Avenue, N.E.
St. Cloud, Minnesota 56301
Programs in prewriting, manuscript, prenumeral, basic concepts, and drawing. Motivation of young children is promoted by use of funform characters.

INSTRUCTIONAL INDUSTRIES, INC.
P.O. Box 13445
Albany, New York 12212
Source for the General Electric/Project Life Pal System, a language improvement system for the preschool exceptional child.

INSTRUCTO/McGRAW-HILL
Paoli, Pennsylvania 19301
Source of small instructional materials and publications for parents and teachers.

JAYFRO

P.O. Box 400

Waterford, Connecticut 6385

Early childhood equipment includes portable obstacle course, a fitness course, fitness equipment, and games materials for little tots.

KAPLAN PRESS

P.O. Box 5128

Winston-Salem, North Carolina 27113

Publishers of LAP (*Learning Accomplishment Profile*) and other materials on assessment, curriculum, parenting, and instruction developed by the Chapel Hill Training-Outreach Project dedicated to the successful education of special children.

KAYE PRODUCTS, INC.

1010 East Pettigrew Street

Durham, North Carolina 27701

Suppliers of adaptive equipment for children.

KIMBO EDUCATIONAL

P.O. Box 477

Long Branch, New Jersey 07740

Albums designed to help young children listen, dance, sing, and learn.

KING FEATURES

Education Division

275 East 45th Street

New York, New York 10017

Fun-in-learning programs include basic reading skills program and language builders.

LET'S PLAY TO GROW

Joseph P. Kennedy, Jr. Foundation

1701 K Street, N.W.

Suite 205

Washington, D.C. 20006

Kit developed to bring the joy of play and shared activities into the lives of parents and their child with special needs. List of low-cost materials available upon request.

LIBIN & ASSOCIATES

907 No. Hollywood Way

Burbank, California 91505

Large equipment for gross motor development and physical fitness.

LONDON BRIDGE

Suite D

7901 Brookford Circle

Baltimore, Maryland 21208

Resource for all kinds of instructional materials equipment and publications for professionals and parents including Academic Therapy Publications.

LOVE PUBLISHING COMPANY

1777 South Bellaire Street

Denver, Colorado 80222

Printed materials for professional development in assessment, instructional planning, and working with parents.

MADDAK INC.

Pequannock, New Jersey 0740

Aids for daily living, home health care, and therapeutic recreation.

MAFEX ASSOCIATES, INC.

90 Cherry Street

Box 519

Johnstown, Pennsylvania 15907

Printed instructional materials for early childhood including complete programs.

MIDWEST PUBLICATIONS

P.O. Box 448

Pacific Grove, California 93950

Source of materials designed to develop thinking skills in primary age or gifted children.

MILTON BRADLEY CO.

Springfield, Massachusetts 01101

Printed and manipulative materials for perception, language, and readiness skills development.

MIRACLE RECREATION EQUIPMENT COMPANY

Hwy. 60 & Bridle Lane

Monnett, Missouri 65708

Play systems designed to cultivate a child's motor skills and physical development. Company supplies planning and funding information assistance.

MODERN EDUCATION CORPORATION

P.O. Box 721

Tulsa, Oklahoma 74101

Comprehensive supply of hardware and software for speech/language and cognitive development, especially designed for use with the gifted.

NASCO LEARNING FUN
901 Janesville Avenue
Fort Atkinson, Wisconsin 53538
or
1524 Princeton Avenue
Modesto, California 95352
School supplies of all kinds, including toddler toys, special education materials, and speech therapy equipment and printed matter.

NEWBY VISUAL LANGUAGE, INC.
Box 121
Eagleville, Pennsylvania 19408
Materials developed to provide teachers and therapists with an extensive collection of illustrations designed to make language visual, for use with handicapped children.

PATHESCOPE EDUCATIONAL MEDIA, INC.
71 Weyman Avenue
New Rochelle, New York 10802
Early childhood media kits for developing gross motor coordination, and staff development series for IEP development.

PITMAN LEARNING, INC.
6 Davis Drive
Belmont, California 94002
Instructional and motivational materials for use with young children; professional materials for writing and implementing IEPs; and assessment materials.

PLAYLEARN
Div. PCA Industries, Inc.
2298 Grissom Drive
St. Louis, Missouri 63141
Large equipment for outdoor and indoor play and therapy.

PRENTKE ROMICH CO.
1022 Heyl Road
Wooster, Ohio 44691
Electronic aids for the severely handicapped, including nonvocal communication aids, environmental control systems, and wheelchair mobility systems.

PRO-ED
5341 Industrial Oaks Blvd.
Austin, Texas 78735
Tests and other publications, including the journal *Topics in Early Childhood Special Education.*

READER'S DIGEST SERVICES, INC.
Educational Division
Pleasantville, New York 10570
Basic readiness and skill builders activities materials.

READING JOY
P.O. Box 404
Naperville, Illinois 60540
Games designed to develop prereading skills.

RESEARCH PRESS
Box 31773
Champaign, Illinois 61821
Printed materials for facilitating language and self-help skills development in young children; also, film catalog.

RHYTHM BAND, INC.
P.O. Box 126
Fort Worth, Texas 76101
Musical instruments adapted for special education and an instructional handbook for teachers.

S & S ARTS AND CRAFTS
Colchester, Connecticut 06415
Supply house of arts and crafts materials with new ideas for therapy, education, and recreation.

SKILLBUILDERS
P.O. Box 376
Irvington, New York 10533
Scooters and other activity equipment for fun, creative play, movement education, and exercise.

SPECIAL LEARNINGS
P.O. Box 23
Streamwood, Illinois 60103
Developers of a comprehensive planbook for special education teachers.

SPELLBINDER
33 Bradford Street
Concord, Massachusetts 01742
Spellbinder in early childhood education helps build basic skills and understanding.

SRA
Science Research Associates, Inc.
155 North Wacker Drive
Chicago, Illinois 60606
DISTAR basal programs in language, reading, and arithmetic for preschool through Grade 3.

STECK–VAUGHN COMPANY
P.O. Box 26015
Austin, Texas 78755
Wide array of instructional materials for the primary age child.

STEP, INC.
P.O. Box 887
8521 44th Avenue West
Mukilteo, Washington 98275
A multisensory, self-correcting learning system for the identification and instruction of children (ages 4–6) with perceptual problems.

TELESENSORY SYSTEMS, INC.
455 N. Bernando Avenue
Mountain View, California 94043
Suppliers of Crib-O-Gram, a neonatal screening audiometer for screening babies with moderately severe to profound hearing loss. Also, equipment for primary age children including the Optacon, a talking calculator, an electronic braille system, the Autacom, and Canon Communicator.

TELEX COMMUNICATIONS, INC.
9600 Aldrich Avenue, South
Minneapolis, Minnesota 55420
Amplification systems designed to reduce background noise for hearing aid users.

TOUCH-STIK PRODUCTS
P.O. Box 5106
136 Fuller Road
Albany, New York 12205
Special material for use in developing eye-hand coordination and teaching sequential relationships.

TREND ENTERPRISES, INC.
P.O. Box 43073
St. Paul, Minnesota 55164
Among a variety of instructional materials are bulletin board sets designed for early childhood education.

UCS, INCORPORATED
155 State Street
Hackensack, New Jersey 07601
Equipment designed to tie cognitive and perceptual development to movement activities.

VORT CORP.
P.O. Box 11552
Palo Alto, California 94306
Publishes *Hawaii Early Learning Profile* (HELP), designed to identify needs and activities from birth to age 3 for developmentally delayed children; and *Behavioral Characteristics Progression* (BCP), a comprehensive criterion-referenced assessment instrument.

WAYNE ENGINEERING
4120 Greenwood Avenue
Skokie, Illinois 60076
Suppliers of The Talking Pen and related products designed to train visual-motor-sensory integration; recommended for use in developmental vision training.

WEBSTER'S INTERNATIONAL, INC.
5729 Cloverland Place
Brentwood, Tennessee 37027
Materials to use with parents for the cognitive and affective development of children.

WEEKLY READER SKILLS BOOK
1250 Fairwood Avenue
P.O. Box 16618
Columbus, Ohio 43216
Basic language arts skills for the primary grade child.

B. L. WINCH & ASSOCIATES
45 Hitching Post Drive, Bldg. 20
Rolling Hills Estates, California 90274
Educational materials for staff development, special education/early childhood, and parent programs.

ZANER–BLOSER
P.O. Box 16764
Columbus, Ohio 43216
Materials for kindergarten; also, kit for determining modality strengths and professional materials.

ZWEIG ASSOCIATES
Div. of Skillcorp, Inc.
1711 McGaw Avenue
Irvine, California 92714

Criterion-referenced tests, diagnostic prescriptive assessment, and classroom management systems for early childhood and special education.

Commercial Catalogs for Self-Help Equipment

Aids for the Special
131 Sayre Street
Elizabeth, New Jersey 07208

BE-OK Self Help Aids
Fred Sammons, Inc.
Box 32
Brookfield, Illinois 60513

CLEO Living Aids
3957 Mayfield road
Cleveland, Ohio 44121

Equipment for Health Care and Rehabilitation
J. A. Preston Corporation
71 Fifth Avenue
New York, New York 10003
(800) 221–2425

Functional Aids for the Multiple Handicapped
United Cerebral Palsy Associations, Inc.
66 East 34th Street
New York, New York 10016

ICTA Catalogue: Aids for Children
(Information Center on Technical Aids)
ICTA Information Center
FACK, S-161 03
Bromma 3, Sweden

Materials for Exceptional Children
J. A. Preston Corporation
71 Fifth Avenue
New York, New York 10003
(800) 221–2425

Skill Development Equipment Company
1340 North Jefferson Street
Anaheim, California 92807

Talon/Velcro Consumer Education
41 E. 51st Street
New York, New York 10022

APPENDIX J
Organizations and Agencies

ACADEMY OF DENTISTRY FOR THE HANDICAPPED (ADH)

211 E. Chicago Avenue

Chicago, Illinois 60611

The Academy of Dentistry for the Handicapped consists of dentists, hygienists, and allied professionals who work to improve the dental care of handicapped persons and encourage dental professionals to treat special patients. Its activities include publications, referral system, continuing education, educational materials clearinghouse, advocacy, and sponsorship of the National Foundation of Dentistry for the Handicapped.

ACCESS AMERICA

Architectural and Transportation Barriers Compliance Board (A&TBCB)

600 3rd Ave., 4th Floor

New York, New York 10016

This agency was created to enforce the Architectural Barriers Act of 1968 that requires physical access for disabled people to and in specified buildings and facilities. A brochure, *Access America*, and a pamphlet, *About Barriers*, provide additional information, including a listing of resources. They are available upon request.

ADMINISTRATION FOR CHILDREN, YOUTH AND FAMILIES (ACYF)

Office of Human Development Services

U.S. Department of Health and Human Services

Washington, D.C. 20201

ACYF is the focal agency within the federal government serving children and families. The agency provides information and assistance to parents, and administers national programs for children and youth, and works with states and communities to develop services that support and strengthen family life. Three major bureaus serve children and families: Head Start Bureau, the Children's

Bureau, and the Youth Development Bureau. Four other offices provide special services to professionals and the public: the Day Care Division; Office on Domestic Violence; Research Demonstration and Evaluation Division; and the Office of Public Information and Education.

ALEXANDER GRAHAM BELL ASSOCIATION FOR THE DEAF

3417 Volta Place, N.W.
Washington, D.C. 20007

The Alexander Graham Bell Association for the Deaf is committed to the idea that hearing impaired children should be afforded the opportunity to develop spoken communication through the effective use of amplified residual hearing and speech skills. It advocates educational options for deaf children and provides consultant services for families pursuing their legal rights. The association publishes and disseminates professional and lay informational materials including audio-visual materials, and sponsors seminars, conferences, and conventions. It maintains a library of works of historical and current importance in the field of deafness.

AMERICAN ALLIANCE FOR HEALTH, PHYSICAL EDUCATION, RECREATION AND DANCE (AAHPERD)
UNIT ON PROGRAMS FOR THE HANDICAPPED

1900 Association Drive
Reston, Virginia 22091

The American Alliance for Health, Physical Education, Recreation, and Dance is a nonprofit organization representing professionals and others involved in health, fitness, sports and related areas. Among its objectives are the production and distribution of educational materials. The alliance provides a strong voice focusing attention on the problems and concerns facing educators and leaders today.

AMERICAN ASSOCIATION OF UNIVERSITY AFFILIATED PROGRAMS FOR THE DEVELOPMENTALLY DISABLED

8630 Fenton St. No. 410
Silver Springs, Maryland 20910

University Affiliated Facilities were established through federal legislation to provide interdisciplinary training for personnel in the field of developmental disabilities; demonstrations of exemplary services; technical assistance; carefully defined adjunctive research; and dissemination of information relating to the provision of such training and services.

AMERICAN ASSOCIATION OF WORKERS FOR THE BLIND

1511 K Street, N.W.
Washington, D.C. 20005

The purpose of this organization is to provide continuing education and information exchange for individuals who work with blind and visually impaired persons.

AMERICAN BROTHERHOOD FOR THE BLIND (ABB)

1800 Johnson Street

Baltimore, Maryland 21230

The American Brotherhood for the Blind, located at the National Center for the Blind, is a charitable and educational foundation serving individuals who are unable to get adequate services from governmental agencies. The ABB produces books for small children and distributes them to blind children, parents, and teachers; develops literature to help people learn about blindness; and provides counseling for the newly blind and their families. Among its publications is a booklet, *Questions Kids Ask about Blindness.*

AMERICAN DIABETES ASSOCIATION, INC.

National Headquarters

1660 Duke St.

Alexandria, Virginia 22314

The goals of the American Diabetes Association are fourfold: patient education programs to help diabetics become effective partners with physicians and other health professionals in understanding, accepting, and caring for their disease; professional education to keep physicians and health professionals abreast of the latest methods of treatment and research; public education to create an awareness of diabetes among the general public of the impact of diabetes on the patient and her or his family; and research to find the cause and ultimately a cure for diabetes. The address of a local affiliate can be found in the Yellow Pages.

AMERICAN FOUNDATION FOR THE BLIND (AFB)

15 W. 16th Street

New York, New York 10011

The American Foundation for the Blind is a private, nonprofit agency established to carry on research, to collect and disseminate information, and to advise and give counsel on matters that improve and strengthen services to blind persons. Among its many services for the blind persons themselves, for the general public, and for the professional: aids and appliances sold at cost, information and referral, travel concession plans, publications, public education, and a library containing one of the largest collections of printed materials on blindness in the world.

AMERICAN OCCUPATIONAL THERAPY ASSOCIATION (AOTA)

1383 Piccard Drive

Rockville, Maryland 20850

The American Occupational Therapy Association (AOTA) promotes quality occupational therapy (OT) services by providing accreditation of educational programs, certification of practitioners, professional development, public education, and advocacy on programs related to national health care issues. AOTA has free professional information packets on subject areas including arthritis, cerebral palsy, and spinal cord injuries. The packets contain the names of resource persons, special facilities, bibliographies of printed material, and selected reprints. State associations provide inquiries with referrals to local OT practitioners and facilities.

AMERICAN PHYSICAL THERAPY ASSOCIATION (APTA)
1111 N. Fairfax Street
Alexandria, Virginia 22314

The goals of the American Physical Therapy Association are the development and improvement of physical therapy education, practice, and research in order to meet the physical therapy needs of people. APTA is mainly a professional organization that serves approximately 31,000 members and publishes the journal, *Physical Therapy*.

AMERICAN PRINTING HOUSE FOR THE BLIND
1839 Frankfort Avenue, P.O. Box 6085
Louisville, Kentucky 40206

The American Printing House for the Blind is the oldest national, nonprofit agency for the blind in the United States and the largest publishing house for the blind in the world. Its activities center around the publication of literature for the visually impaired, including textbooks and other educational materials; the development and manufacture of educational aids and appliances for their use; educational and technical research relating to publishing literature for the visually impaired; and the manufacture of tangible aids for the use of the visually handicapped.

AMERICAN RED CROSS
431 18th St., N.W.
Washington, D.C. 20006

Known for its efforts to improve the quality of human life through a variety of services, the American Red Cross also promotes adapted aquatic programs to meet the needs of individuals who, because of a mental or physical impairment, cannot readily achieve success in a regular swimming program. The benefits for the participants of adapted aquatic programs include increased strength, a sense of achievement, and opportunities for group participation. Other areas of instruction include first aid, home nursing, care of young children (for teenagers), and parenting.

AMERICAN SPEECH-LANGUAGE-HEARING ASSOCIATION (ASHA)
10801 Rockville Pike
Rockville, Maryland 20852

The American Speech-Language-Hearing Association (ASHA) is the national scientific and professional association for speech-language pathologists and audiologists concerned with communication behavior and disorders. Its goals are to maintain high standards of clinical competence for professionals providing services to the public; to encourage the development of comprehensive clinical service programs; to promote investigation of clinical procedures used in treating disorders of communication; to stimulate exchange of information about human communication; and to encourage basic research and scientific study of human communication and its disorders.

ARTHRITIS FOUNDATION
1314 Spring St., N.W.
Atlanta, Georgia 30309

The Arthritis Foundation is the only national, voluntary health association seeking the total answer—cause, prevention, and cure—to the #1 crippling disease. It exists to provide help to persons with arthritis and their doctors through programs of research, patient service, public health information and education, professional education, and training. Of interest to parents and teachers are two publications: *Arthritis in Children* and *When Your Student Has Childhood Arthritis: A Guide for Teachers.*

ASSOCIATION FOR CHILDHOOD EDUCATION INTERNATIONAL (ACEI)
11501 Georgia Ave., Suite 312
Wheaton, Maryland 20902

The Association for Childhood Education International is concerned for all children from infancy through early adolescence. At the present time, its purposes focus on three action areas including: (1) enhancing the quality of family life; (2) improving the educational climate for children; and (3) developing an effective public information network. The goals and aspirations of ACEI are expressed through its journal, *Childhood Education,* and numerous publications that reflect research and broad-based viewpoints about a wide range of issues affecting children.

ASSOCIATION FOR CHILDREN AND ADULTS WITH LEARNING DISABILITIES (ACLD)
4156 Library Road
Pittsburgh, Pennsylvania 15234

ACLD is the only national organization devoted to defining and finding solutions for the broad spectrum of learning problems. Its goals include encouraging research in neurophysiological and psychological aspects of learning disabilities; stimulating development of early detection programs; creating a climate of public awareness and acceptance; disseminating information; serving as an advocate; developing and promoting legislative assistance; and improving regular and special education.

ASSOCIATION FOR EDUCATION & REHABILITATION OF THE VISUALLY IMPAIRED

206 N. Washington St., Suite 320
Alexandria, Virginia 22314

The Association for Education of the Visually Handicapped is a professional organization that provides information through publication, conferences and meetings, youth education activities, and clearinghouse service. Through the central office, an attempt is made to provide reference and informational material to members, administrators, parents, and others interested in visually handicapped children.

ASSOCIATION FOR RETARDED CITIZENS OF THE U.S. (ARC)

National Headquarters
500 E. Border St., Suite 300
Arlington, Texas 76010

The Association for Retarded Citizens is a national organization of volunteers (parents, educators, and professionals in the field) devoted to improving the welfare of all mentally retarded persons. The organization provides help to parents, individuals, organizations, and communities to solve the problems brought about by mental retardation. Its work includes fostering research on prevention and effective educational techniques, public awareness in all areas of mental retardation, progressive legislation, and reminding all concerned that retarded persons are entitled to the full range of human and civil rights. Addresses of local chapters may be secured from ARC.

THE ASSOCIATION FOR THE GIFTED (TAG)

The Council for Exceptional Children
1920 Association Drive
Reston, Virginia 22091

The purposes of this division within the Council for Exceptional Children are to disseminate information and encourage research and scholarly investigation relevant to the problems of the gifted; to encourage professional training for teachers and others who work with the gifted; to advance standards for professional training and for school programs for the gifted; and to cooperate with other agencies and organizations in efforts related to the education and welfare of the gifted.

THE ASSOCIATION FOR THE SEVERELY HANDICAPPED (TASH)

7010 Roosevelt Way NE
Seattle, Washington 98115

TASH works to improve the quality of life for severely handicapped individuals through advocacy and through the dissemination of information via a monthly newsletter, quarterly journal, annual conference, local chapters, and information department. The organization encourages an effective use of all disciplines and of all interested people: parents, teachers, administrators, medical personnel, OT/ PTs, and all others who must share expertise and experience in order to achieve the goals supported by TASH.

ASTHMA AND ALLERGY FOUNDATION OF AMERICA

1125 15th St., N.W., Suite 502
Washington, DC 20005

The Asthma and Allergy Foundation of America seeks to educate the public regarding asthma and allergies through pamphlets and films, supports research and training in allergy and immunology through grants, and provides activities through local chapters. Among the many publications of this organization is a pamphlet entitled, *Tips for Teachers.*

BUREAU OF HEALTH EDUCATION AND AUDIOVISUAL SERVICES
AMERICAN DENTAL ASSOCIATION

211 East Chicago Avenue
Chicago, Illinois 60611

The focus of this component of the American Dental Association is the dissemination of educational materials for parents and other lay persons and professionals who work with handicapped children. Those interested may secure the annual catalog of printed and audiovisual materials and a mimeographed *Resource List on Dentistry for the Handicapped* that also identifies other dental organizations offering services for handicapped children and their families.

THE CANADIAN NATIONAL INSTITUTE FOR THE BLIND

1931 Bayview Avenue
M4G 4C8
Toronto, Ontario, Canada

The major focus of this agency is to provide a program of rehabilitation and support services to help blind people help themselves, and to work to prevent blindness through educational materials and activities.

CHILD DEVELOPMENT CLINIC

University Hospital School
The University of Iowa
Iowa City, Iowa 52242

The primary role of the Child Development Clinic is to serve as a diagnostic clinic for developmental, learning, and behavioral problems in children. Once problems are delineated, the child is referred to the personal physician and the resources of the local community with appropriate recommendations. In selected cases, short-term therapy may be provided by the clinic. Similar services may be provided in other comprehensive university centers.

CHILD WELFARE LEAGUE OF AMERICA, INC.

440 1st St., N.W., Suite 310

Washington, D.C. 20001

The Child Welfare League of America is a standard-setting federation of 400 leading child welfare agencies in the United States and Canada, public and private, religious and nonsectarian. Its sole reason for existence is to improve services to children. It speaks for the approximately 12 million children in the United States and Canada who are seriously deprived, neglected, and abused. Publications and training programs are its primary means of disseminating information. The league provides no direct services to children or their parents. Instead, it serves the agency that serves the child.

CHILDREN IN HOSPITALS (CIH)

31 Wilshire Park

Needham, Massachusetts 02192

Children in Hospitals is a nonprofit organization of parents and health care professionals. It seeks to educate all those concerned about the needs of children and parents for continued and frequent contact when either is hospitalized. An information brochure is available on request.

CLOSER LOOK

Box 1492

Washington, D.C. 20013

As a national resource center, Closer Look helps parents of handicapped children by providing information on state and federal laws and advice concerning parents' rights and responsibilities. It encourages the coalition of parent organizations for promoting and maintaining the implementation of mandated programs. Closer Look is a project of the Parents' Campaign for Handicapped Children and Youth.

CLOTHING RESEARCH AND DEVELOPMENT FOUNDATION (CRDF)

P.O. Box 347

Milford, New Jersey 08848

CRDF was founded to help alleviate the clothing problems of the physically handicapped. The organization educates and consults with designers and manufacturers on clothing designs that permit handicapped persons to dress themselves without aid or with minimal aid.

COLUMBIA UNIVERSITY
SCHOOL OF DENTAL AND ORAL SURGERY

Div. of Pedodontics

630 W. 168th Street

New York, New York 10032

The Columbia University School of Dental and Oral Surgery has a clinic for handicapped patients, including children. In the clinic both preventive and corrective oral health care are made available, and special techniques for toothbrushing and oral hygiene maintenance are presented. Emphasis is placed on the necessary role of the parent in active oral hygiene care. Similar services may be provided by the school of dentistry in a comprehensive university.

CONFERENCE OF EXECUTIVES OF AMERICAN SCHOOLS FOR THE DEAF (CEASD)

5034 Wisconsin Avenue, N.W.
Washington, D.C. 20016

CEASD is a copublisher of *American Annals of the Deaf* and informational brochures. It conducts an annual convention and workshops throughout the year. As an advocate, it establishes and promotes standards for educational programs and related services, expresses member views on legislation, and accredits schools and programs for the deaf. This organization provides information regarding deaf education and refers inquiries to more appropriate information services when necessary.

CONVENTION OF AMERICAN INSTRUCTORS OF THE DEAF (CAID)

C/O Dr. Stephanie Polowe
Office of the President
P.O. Box 9887, LBJ 2264
Rochester, New York 14623–0887

Categories of services include professional publication, professional development, advocacy for legislation and services to benefit education of the deaf, information services, and production of educational materials for dissemination. Membership is open to anyone actively involved in the education of the deaf and to those in related services.

COUNCIL FOR CHILDREN WITH BEHAVIORAL DISORDERS (CCBD)

The Council for Exceptional Children
1920 Association Drive
Reston, Virginia 22091–1589

The purposes of this division within the Council for Exceptional Children are to develop lines of communication and interaction among professionals, disciplines, and organizations; to promote adequate programs for recruitment, training, and consultation; to promote research and development; and to support legislation for services to behaviorally disordered children.

COUNCIL FOR EDUCATIONAL DIAGNOSTIC SERVICES (CEDS)

The Council for Exceptional Children
1920 Association Drive
Reston, Virginia 22091–1589

The purposes of this division within the Council for Exceptional Children are to promote the most appropriate education of children and youth through appraisal, diagnosis, educational intervention, implementation, and continuous evaluation of a prescribed educational program; to facilitate the integration of services offered by educational diagnosticians, psychologists, social workers, physicians, and/or other disciplines; and to promote research that encourages the evolution of more efficient diagnostic instruments, practices, and techniques leading to a better understanding of the relationship between educational needs and educational practices.

THE COUNCIL FOR EXCEPTIONAL CHILDREN (CEC)
1920 Association Drive
Reston, Virginia 22091

The Council for Exceptional Children is an international organization of individuals (mostly professionals in special education) concerned with quality education for handicapped and gifted children. Its members benefit from the following offerings: opportunity for involvement with special interest groups; special services, including publications, extensive information service, group insurance, discounts on publications, and economy travel programs; professional growth for educators through conventions, conferences, and institutes; and effective government interaction. CEC divisions are organizations within the Council for Exceptional Children. Divisions of interest to parents and teachers of young handicapped and gifted children include: the Council for Children with Behavioral Disorders (CCBD); Division on Mental Retardation (CEC-MR); Council for Educational Diagnostic Services (CEDS); Division for Children with Communication Disorders (DCCD); Division for Children with Learning Disabilities (DCLD); Division for Early Childhood (DEC); Division for Physically Handicapped (DPH); Division for the Visually Handicapped (DVH); the Association for the Gifted (TAG); and Teacher Education Division (TED). These are included by name in this listing of resources.

CYSTIC FIBROSIS FOUNDATION (CF)
6931 Arlington Road, No. 200
Bethesda, Maryland 20814

The mission of the Cystic Fibrosis Foundation is to find the means for prevention, control, and effective treatment of cystic fibrosis. The goal of the foundation is to improve the length of survival and quality of life for individuals affected by CF, and to reduce the impact of the disease on the patient, family, and society. CF publishes *A Teacher's Guide to Cystic Fibrosis*, available upon request.

DEAFNESS RESEARCH FOUNDATION (DRF)
9 East 38th Street
New York, New York 10016

The DRF informs the public on deafness and ear disease and provides a means of contributing financially to the advances of research on causes, prevention, and treatment. The DRF annually funds 35 to 40 grants in support of new research throughout the United States and Canada. It also directs and partially finances the National Temporal Bone Bank Program, the donor program in the field of deafness and hearing impairment. This program provides internal auditory structures badly needed in medical training and ear research.

DIVISION FOR CHILDREN WITH COMMUNICATION DISORDERS (DCCD)
The Council for Exceptional Children
1920 Association Drive
Reston, Virginia 22091

The purposes of this division within the Council for Exceptional Children are to promote the education of children with communication disorders and to encourage and promote professional growth and research as a means of creating better understanding of the problems related to children with communication disorders.

DIVISION FOR CHILDREN WITH LEARNING DISABILITIES (DCLD)
The Council for Exceptional Children
1920 Association Drive
Reston, Virginia 22091

The purpose of this division within the Council for Exceptional Children is to promote the education and general welfare of children with specific learning disabilities through improving teacher preparation programs, improving local special education programs, resolving research issues, and coordinating activities with other CEC divisions and with professional organizations outside the council structure.

DIVISION FOR EARLY CHILDHOOD (DEC)
The Council for Exceptional Children
1920 Association Drive
Reston, Virginia 22091

The purposes of this division within the Council for Exceptional Children are to promote the education of all exceptional youth and infants; to promote programs that cooperatively involve parents in their children's education; to stimulate communication and joint activity among early childhood organizations; and to disseminate information through publications, workshops, and professional meetings.

DIVISION FOR THE PHYSICALLY HANDICAPPED (DPH)
The Council for Exceptional Children
1920 Association Drive
Reston, Virginia 22091

The purposes of this division within the Council for Exceptional Children are to promote a closer professional relationship among educators of children and

youth who are homebound or hospitalized or in classes for the physically handicapped; to encourage the study of new ideas, practices, and techniques and to
disseminate this information through professional meetings, workshops, and
publications; and to initiate and cooperate in research or demonstration projects
and studies.

DIVISION FOR THE VISUALLY HANDICAPPED (DVH)
The Council for Exceptional Children
1920 Association Drive
Reston, Virginia 22091

The purposes of this division within the Council for Exceptional Children are to
advance the education and training of children and youth with visual handicaps
that impede their educational progress; to bring about a better understanding of
the educational, emotional, or related problems that may be associated with
visual handicaps; to encourage the study of new ideas, practices, and techniques;
and to disseminate this information through professional meetings, workshops,
and publications.

DIVISION ON MENTAL RETARDATION (CEC-MR)
The Council for Exceptional Children
c/o Dr. Dana M. Anderson
245 Cedar Springs Drive
Athens, Georgia 30605

The purposes of this division within the Council for Exceptional Children are to
advance the educational and general welfare of the mentally retarded, research in
the education of the mentally retarded, competency of educators engaged in the
field, public understanding of mental retardation, and legislation needed to help
accomplish these goals; and to encourage and promote professional growth,
research, and the dissemination and utilization of research findings.

DOWN SYNDROME CONGRESS
1640 W. Roosevelt Road
R156E
Chicago, Illinois 60608

A group of parents and professionals share their experiences with other parents,
physicians, and educators, and work for public awareness and acceptance of the
Down syndrome child. At local levels, members seek out parents of infants with
Down syndrome to put them in touch with the family support network and to
encourage them and to instruct them in early home educational methods. Published material and answers to inquiries are available on request.

EPILEPSY FOUNDATION OF AMERICA (EFA)
4351 Garden City Drive
Landover, Maryland 20785

The EFA is a national voluntary health organization that advocates for the over 2 million persons with epilepsy in the United States. Its service components include a client services department information and education, legal advocacy, government liaison, and chapter-field services. Pamphlets of interest to students and teachers of the preschool handicapped include *The Epilepsy School Alert, The Teacher's Role*, and *Teacher Tips about Epilepsies*, available at nominal cost.

ERIC CLEARINGHOUSE ON HANDICAPPED AND GIFTED CHILDREN
The Council for Exceptional Children
1920 Association Drive
Reston, Virginia 22091

The clearinghouse collects, abstracts, and indexes English language literature on the education of handicapped and gifted children. Publications and services include fact sheet, spot bibliographies, custom computer searches, computer search reprints, referrals, and a variety of publications.

FAMILY SERVICE ASSOCIATION OF AMERICA, INC.
44 East 23rd Street
New York, New York 10010

Since its beginning in 1911, the Family Service Association of America has been at the center of a voluntary movement to strengthen family life. Through programs of research, training and technical assistance, the movement has increased its knowledge and its capability to help families confronted by a wide range of problems. Actions and services to prevent family problems include an extensive publication program, public education efforts, and cooperative activities with other family-oriented organizations.

GESELL INSTITUTE OF HUMAN DEVELOPMENT
310 Prospect Street
New Haven, Connecticut 06511

The Gesell Institute offers visual, psychological, and medical services to children. In addition to research into the way in which human behavior develops and into ways in which the individual's health and/or behavior can be improved, the institute offers clinical help for any child in trouble. Its orientation is primarily biological, advocating the grouping of children according to behavioral maturation instead of chronological age. A list of publications and services may be requested by phone or mail.

HEAD START
Administration for Children, Youth and Families
Office of Human Development Services
U.S. Department of Health and Human Services, P.O. Box 1182
Washington, D.C. 20013

Head Start is a major program (with bureau status) within the Administration for Children, Youth and Families, U.S. Dept. of Health and Human Services. From its beginning, Head Start has been an innovative, experimental demonstration program that has had a strong impact on communities and early childhood programs across the country. There are four major components in Project Head Start including: education; health (medical and dental, nutrition, and mental health); parent involvement; and social services. This project has generated numerous publications used in programs for the preschool handicapped.

INSTITUTE FOR CHILD BEHAVIOR RESEARCH
4157 Adams Avenue
San Diego, California 92116

The primary purpose of the institute is to conduct, encourage, and disseminate the results of research related to severe behavior disorders in childhood, such as autism, childhood schizophrenia, or so-called severe emotional disturbance. The institute conducts most of its business by mail. It corresponds with parents, professionals, teachers, and researchers interested in children with autism and similar disorders. In recent years research has centered around nutritional approaches to the amelioration of childhood behavior disorders.

INSTITUTE OF LOGOPEDICS
2400 Jardine Drive
Wichita, Kansas 67219

Programs at the Institute of Logopedics emphasize the development of communication skills.

INTERNATIONAL ASSOCIATION OF LIONS CLUBS
300 22nd Street
Oak Brook, Illinois 60521

This is an international association of business and professional men with a major service interest in the visually handicapped. This address may be used to secure the names of local clubs and contact persons who can, in turn, supply information on the services they provide.

INTERNATIONAL ASSOCIATION OF PARENTS OF THE DEAF (IAPD)
814 Thayer Avenue
Silver Spring, Maryland 20910

IAPD provides information about deafness to parents and the general public and refers parents to local contacts when appropriate. A newsletter, *The Endeavor*, is published six times a year. Free copies of *The Endeavor* may be requested. IAPD has developed position papers on a variety of subjects to give members support and guidance in areas of vital concern to parents. Speakers are available for meetings, seminars, and conventions.

INTERNATIONAL READING ASSOCIATION (IRA)

800 Barksdale Road
P.O. Box 8139
Newark, Delaware 19714

The International Reading Association is a professional organization interested in improving reading instruction. It encourages study of the reading process, research, and better teacher education and promotes the development of reading proficiency. The association's goals are furthered through publications, meetings and conventions, and councils and affiliates that work to improve literacy at all levels.

JOHN F. KENNEDY INSTITUTE

707 North Broadway
Baltimore, Maryland 21205

This institute provides comprehensive diagnostic and treatment services for handicapped children from birth to 21 years of age. Services include pediatrics, dentistry, psychology, special education, hearing and speech, occupational therapy, physical therapy, and nutrition.

JOHN TRACY CLINIC

806 West Adams Blvd.
Los Angeles, California 90007

The clinic's goals are to find, encourage, guide, and train the parents of young deaf children, first to reach and help the children understand language and speak, and second to help the parents themselves.

LEGAL SERVICES CORPORATION

733 15th Street, N.W.
Washington, D.C. 20005

The Legal Services Corporation was set up by Congress to support local legal services for the poor. The institute also conducts seminars and meetings on topics that affect the law and on services needed by the poor.

LEUKEMIA SOCIETY OF AMERICA

600 3rd Avenue
New York, New York 10016

The Leukemia Society of America is a voluntary health agency that concentrates its efforts on finding the cause and eventual cure for leukemia. It has a three-pronged program of research, patient aid, and public and professional education. Of these, its main thrust is research.

MARCH OF DIMES BIRTH DEFECTS FOUNDATION
1275 Mamaroneck Avenue

White Plains, New York 10605

In seeking the prevention of birth defects, the March of Dimes supports programs of research, medical service, and professional and public health education. The foundation's work is directed primarily at overcoming those birth defects that claim infant lives or substantially interfere with the ability of an individual to lead a normal life.

MENTAL HEALTH MATERIALS CENTER (MHMC)
P.O. Box 304

Bronxville, New York 10708

MHMC was established to facilitate effective dissemination and utilization of proven mental health program aids including publication, films, techniques, and ideas for the purpose of assisting mental health program planners. The organizational goals are accomplished through collaboration with other agencies, and providing professionals with material, seminars, workshops, and continuing education.

MENTAL RETARDATION ASSOCIATION OF AMERICA (MRAA)
211 East 3rd South, Suite 212

Salt Lake City, Utah 84111

The association is an independent volunteer organization dedicated to serving the nation's mentally retarded and developmentally disabled children and adults. It is an advocate at the national, state, and local levels promoting a moderate, yet realistic, approach to the whole field of mental retardation.

MUSCULAR DYSTROPHY ASSOCIATION (MDA)
3300 E. Sunrise Drive

Tucon, Arizona 85718

The Muscular Dystrophy Association is a voluntary national health agency, a dedicated partnership between scientists and concerned citizens aimed at conquering neuromuscular diseases and fostering research and patient care. The work of this organization is accomplished through: (1) basic and applied research; (2) comprehensive programs of patient services and clinical care; and (3) widespread professional and public education. Among its many publications is a booklet, *Around the Clock Aids for the Child with Muscular Dystrophy*, available upon request.

NATIONAL ASSOCIATION FOR THE EDUCATION OF YOUNG CHILDREN (NAEYC)
1834 Connecticut Avenue, N.W.

Washington, D.C. 20009

The expressed purpose of the National Association for the Education of Young Children is to serve and act on behalf of the needs and rights of young children, with primary focus on the provision of educational services and resources, including the publication of books and a journal, *Young Children*, to adults who work with and for children. Founded in 1926, NAEYC has grown to an organization of more than 32,000 members involved in a wide range of early childhood services.

NATIONAL ASSOCIATION FOR THE VISUALLY HANDICAPPED (NAVH)
22 W. 21st Street
New York, New York 10010

The National Association for the Visually Handicapped provides service to the low-vision child, the parents, and professionals and paraprofessionals working with the partially seeing child. Services include informational literature, referral to local sources of assistance, counsel, and guidance. California residents should contact the NAVH office at 3201 Balboa Street, San Francisco, California 94121.

NATIONAL ASSOCIATION OF PRIVATE RESIDENTIAL FACILITIES FOR THE MENTALLY RETARDED (NAPRFMR)
6269 Leesburg Pike, Suite B-5
Falls Church, Virginia 22044

NAPRFMR is an association of providers of private residential services for people who are developmentally disabled. Its major focus is upon federal legislation and regulations that impact on the delivery of those services. Other services to member agencies include group insurance and training for providers through workshops and seminars held around the country each year. NAPRFMR also provides referral information to persons seeking appropriate residential placement for a disabled person.

NATIONAL ASSOCIATION OF STATE MENTAL RETARDATION PROGRAMS DIRECTORS, INC. (NASMRPD)
113 Oronoco Street
Alexandria, Virginia 22314

NASMRPD is the spokesman for the interests of state mental retardation agencies in the halls of Congress and among federal agencies. In addition, the association maintains continuous contact with legislators to assure that the membership are fully considered. It serves as a clearinghouse for the sharing/exchange of information on programming and legislation for the MR/DD population to insure more appropriate/effective service delivery.

NATIONAL ASSOCIATION FOR THE DEAF (NAD)
814 Thayer Avenue
Silver Spring, Maryland 20910

NAD serves as a clearinghouse of information on deafness and as an advocate of civil rights for deaf individuals. The association conducts research and supports related research in areas involving deafness. Its publications include over 220 books on various aspects of deafness (parent education, psychology, mental health, children's books, etc.).

NATIONAL ATAXIA FOUNDATION (NAF)
750 Twelve Oaks Center
Wayzata, Minnesota 55391

The National Ataxia Foundation (NAF) is a nonprofit, charitable organization concerned with all types of hereditary ataxia and related conditions, including peroneal muscular atrophy, spastic paraplegia, ataxia telangiectasia and hereditary tremor. Its objectives are: (1) location of patients and persons at risk; (2) increased awareness about hereditary disorders; (3) prevention of the spread of these disorders; and (4) research.

NATIONAL CENTER FOR CLINICAL INFANT PROGRAMS
733 15th Street, N.W., Suite 912
Washington, D.C. 20005

The center was established by leaders in the fields of pediatrics research and clinical practice, child development and related disciplines to improve and support professional initiatives in infant mental health and development. It accomplishes these goals through its programs: fellowships, training conferences for professionals, liaison with other child-related private and government agencies.

THE NATIONAL CENTER FOR LAW AND THE DEAF
7th and Florida Avenue, N.W.
Washington, D.C. 20002

The National Center for Law and the Deaf has been established to develop and provide a variety of legal services to the deaf community, including representation, counseling, information and education. The center offers these services: free individual legal counseling on issues such as social security, landlord/tenant, welfare, and insurance; national programs, including workshops on legal rights; information packets on new laws or proposed legislation; and police cards to explain the special problems of the deaf. The National Center for Law and the Deaf is located at and sponsored by Gallaudet College.

NATIONAL CHILDREN'S CENTER, INC.
6200 Second Street, N.W.
Washington, D.C. 20011

The National Children's Center, Inc. is a private, nonprofit, nonsectarian, and nondiscriminatory agency offering residential and day care to children, adolescents, and young adults handicapped by mental retardation and other developmental disabilities. Programs include educational diagnosis and prescription, casework services, medical and dental care, physical therapy, prevocation, psychological, psychiatric, and language development services, research, professional and paraprofessional training. A preschool integrated classroom and infant stimulation program are available.

NATIONAL COUNCIL ON FAMILY RELATIONS (NCFR)
3989 Central Avenue
Minneapolis, Minnesota 55421

The NCFR is an international nonprofit educational and resource organization dedicated to the strengthening of the family. The goal of the council is to assist professionals in developing professional standards in the field. The membership of the council is comprised of researchers, clinical practitioners in family therapy, and professionals in related disciplines. The main information component of the council is the Family Resource and Referral Center (FRRC).

NATIONAL EASTER SEAL SOCIETY
70 E. Lake Street
Chicago, Illinois 60601

The National Easter Seal Society, headquarters for the federation of local and state organizations, conducts national public awareness, disseminates information, and awards grants for research into causes, treatment, and rehabilitation of disabling conditions. It publishes a variety of books, pamphlets, and reprints for professionals, parents, and persons with disabilities. Subjects of interest to those working with young children include advocacy, attitudes, barrier-free environment, dental care, self-help, education, prevention, social and psychological aspects, and volunteers. For additional information, contact the program service department.

NATIONAL FEDERATION OF THE BLIND (NFB)
National Center for the Blind
1800 Johnson Street
Baltimore, Maryland 21230

The National Federation of the Blind is the organization of the blind in America. Interested sighted persons are also welcome to join. Long-range purposes include integrating blind persons into American society so they are seen as normal, participating citizens, and showing blind children there can be a full life waiting for them. Work toward these goals includes ensuring that training in the techniques necessary to function efficiently without sight is available; helping blind persons find jobs; and endeavoring to change outmoded laws, regulations, and practices that prevent blind people form normal living. NFB provides support services to newly blinded persons and to the parents of children born blind. One of its many publications is *A Reference Guide for Parents and Educators of Blind Children*, available through the organization.

NATIONAL HEARING AID SOCIETY
20361 Middlebelt Road
Livonia, Michigan 48152

The National Hearing Aid Society is a nonprofit professional association of hearing aid specialists who test hearing for the selection, fitting, adaptation, counseling, instruction, repair, sales, and service of hearing aids.

THE NATIONAL HEMOPHILIA FOUNDATION
110 Greene Street, Suite 303
New York, New York 10012

The National Hemophilia Foundation (NHF), a voluntary nonprofit health organization, seeks solutions to the various aspects of the hemophilia problem. Its activities progress along three lines: (1) helping the hemophiliac and his or her family; (2) seeking the eventual cure and elimination of the disease; and (3) using national blood resources effectively. Each of the more than 50 chapters has a medical advisory committee to promote high standards of care and efficient use of community blood resources.

NATIONAL INSTITUTE OF CHILD HEALTH AND HUMAN DEVELOPMENT
Office of Research Reporting
Dept. of Health and Human Services
Public Health Service
National Institutes of Health
Bethesda, Maryland 20205

The National Institute of Child Health and Human Development (NICHD) is an institution that supports and conducts research in the biomedical, behavioral, and social sciences and produces publications that are primarily research reports, available in single copy distribution. These include reprints of articles from professional journals, special topical reports, and other professional literature. A list of available publications may be obtained upon request.

NATIONAL LIBRARY SERVICE FOR THE BLIND AND PHYSICALLY HANDICAPPED (NSL)
Library of Congress
Washington, D.C. 20542

A free national library program of braille, large-print, and recorded materials for the blind and physically handicapped adults and children is administered by NSL. With the cooperation of authors and publishers who grant permission to use copyrighted works, NSL selects and produces full-length books, magazines, and other materials in braille and on recorded disc and cassette. Reading and music materials are distributed to a network of libraries where they are circulated to eligible borrowers by postage-free mail. Additionally, an information service on various aspects of blindness and physical handicaps is available without charge to individuals, organizations, and libraries. NSL also sponsors research and development projects directed to reducing costs for books and equipment, speeding delivery of materials to borrowers, and improving the quality of materials and services.

NATIONAL MEDIA MATERIALS CENTER FOR SEVERELY HANDICAPPED PERSONS

George Peabody College
Box 318
Vanderbilt University
Nashville, Tennessee 37203

Goals of this organization include reviewing currently available media materials for severely handicapped persons, their teachers, their aides, and their parents; analyzing areas where no materials are available; adapting or developing materials to fill areas of need; and holding an annual symposium to share instructional technological information in the area of education of the severely handicapped.

NATIONAL MENTAL HEALTH ASSOCIATION

1021 Prince Street
Alexandria, Virginia 22314–2971

The National Mental Health Association is a nationwide voluntary, nongovernmental organization dedicated to the promotion of mental health, the prevention of mental illness, and the improved care and treatment of the mentally ill. Its 850 chapters and divisions and more than 1 million citizen volunteers work toward these goals through a wide range of activities in social action, education, advocacy, and information.

NATIONAL RESOURCE CENTER FOR PARAPROFESSIONALS IN SPECIAL EDUCATION

Center for Advance Study in Education: New Careers Training Laboratory
33 West 42nd Street
New York, New York 10036

The purpose of the center is to promote an increase in the use of trained paraprofessionals in special education. Information is provided for the use of employers, program managers, and trainers on such issues as skills and competencies needed by paraprofessionals, new roles for paraprofessionals in educational programs, credentialing, and career mobility. It also provides information on in-service training models and training materials in use by state and local education agencies and by institutions of higher education.

NATIONAL RETINITIS PIGMENTOSA FOUNDATION

8331 Mindale Circle

Baltimore, Maryland 21207

The major goals of the foundation are to support research to discover the cause, prevention, and treatment of retinal degenerative diseases such as retinitis pigmentosa (RP), Usher's syndrome, and macular degeneration; and to provide information and referral to all people affected by these blinding heritable diseases. Additionally, the foundation sponsors the RP Donor Program.

NATIONAL SOCIETY FOR AUTISTIC CHILDREN (NSAC)

Suite #1017

1234 Massachusetts Avenue, N.W.

Washington, D.C. 20005

The National Society for Autistic Children is the only national agency dedicated to the education and welfare of people with autism. Its priorities are research and education. Through more than 100 chapters across the United States, it collects and disseminates information.

NATIONAL SOCIETY TO PREVENT BLINDNESS (NSPB)

500 E. Remington Road

Schaumburg, Illinois 60173

This organization works to prevent blindness by sponsoring community screening and testing programs, public and professional education, and research. Community programs, carried out through 25 affiliated volunteer state agencies, concentrate on health education and free screening for the public. NSPB provides answers by mail to specific questions about eye disease, eye safety, vision defects, and eye checkups.

NATIONAL SPINAL CORD INJURY FOUNDATION

369 Elliot Street

Newton Upper Falls, Massachusetts 02164

The foundation addresses the needs of individuals with spinal cord injuries and their families through its goals of care, cure, and coping. Through its programs the foundation seeks to insure comprehensive systems of quality care for persons who have spinal cord injuries and to provide educational and informational services.

NATIONAL TAY-SACHS AND ALLIED DISEASES ASSOCIATION

2001 Beacon Street

Brookline, MA 02146

The National Tay-Sachs and Allied Diseases Association is an organization of parents and physicians founded for the purpose of combating genetic diseases that kill infants and children. The association concentrates its efforts on support services for victims and their families by working with governmental agencies, civic groups, and medical institutions to promote community-based programs for prevention. Through seminars, conferences, and publications, information is disseminated to health agencies for them to benefit from and make use of the organization's efforts concerning diseases for which Tay-Sachs is a prototype.

NEW EYES FOR THE NEEDY

P.O. Box 332
549 Millburn Avenue
Short Hills, New Jersey 07078

This organization provides funds for new prescription glasses, artificial eyes, and lenticular contact lenses to medically indigent persons who are not eligible for other sources of financial assistance. Information about qualifying for financial assistance is provided.

OFFICE OF INFORMATION AND RESOURCES FOR THE HANDICAPPED

Clearinghouse on the Handicapped
Office of Special Education and Rehabilitative Services (OSERS)
Department of Education
Room 3106, Switzer Building
Washington, D.C. 20202

This office is predominately a clearinghouse and information service. If it cannot supply a direct answer, the inquirer is referred to appropriate information sources. Its publication, Directory of *National Sources on Handicapping Conditions and Related Services*, describes organizations with capabilities and competencies in the field.

OFFICE FOR MATERNAL AND CHILD HEALTH

Bureau of Community Health Services
Health Services Administration, HHS
5600 Fishers Lane
Rockville, Maryland 20857

The purposes of this agency are: (1) to extend and improve services for reducing infant mortality and otherwise improving the health of mothers and children; and (2) to locate and provide diagnosis, medical, surgical, and corrective care, including hospitalization and after care for children who are crippled or suffer from conditions leading to crippling. Emphasis is given to economically disadvantaged and rural areas. Programs cover all states and jurisdictions. A listing of publications is available.

ORTON DYSLEXIA SOCIETY, INC.

Chester Bldg., Suite 382

8600 LaSalle Road

Baltimore, Maryland 21286–2044

This is an international organization that disseminates information on specific language disabilities (dyslexia). No clinical or educational facilities are offered. It provides guidance and resource services in Canada, Bermuda, and the United States.

PARENTS OF DOWN'S SYNDROME CHILDREN

c/o Montgomery Co. Assn. for Retarded Citizens

11600 Nebel Street

Rockville, MD 20852

PODS provides conversation, exchange of information, and mutual support for parents of children with Down syndrome through meetings and an information packet for new parents.

PRADER-WILLI SYNDROME ASSOCIATION

5515 Malibu Drive

Edina, Minnesota 55436

This association was formed to provide a vehicle of communication for parents, professionals and other interested citizens. It is dedicated to the sharing of experiences in how to cope with this syndrome. It is a nonprofit organization founded because of the lack of materials available to people with this syndrome. A bimonthly newsletter, *The Gathered View*, is the primary communication medium for the organization.

RECORDING FOR THE BLIND, INC.

20 Roszel Road

Princeton, NJ 08540

Recording for the Blind (RFB) is a national, nonprofit, voluntary organization that provides recorded educational books, free on loan, to individuals who cannot read normal printed material because of visual, physical, or perceptual handicaps. RFB's services are fundamental aids to handicapped students at all levels as well as to those who require educational or specialized materials in the pursuit of their occupations. Materials can be borrowed for a period of one year on a free loan basis. Further information may be obtained through direct correspondence.

SCHOOL PROGRAMS DIVISION

Food and Nutrition Service (FNS)

U.S. Department of Agriculture

Washington, D.C. 20250

The Food and Nutrition Service of the U.S. Department of Agriculture administers child nutrition programs in cooperation with state and local governments.

Together, they work to safeguard the health and well-being of the nation's children. The programs serve eligible children in public and nonprofit private schools, child care centers, settlement houses, summer camps, recreation centers, and other eligible institutions.

SPINA BIFIDA ASSOCIATION OF AMERICA (SBAA)

4590 Mac Arthur Blvd., N.W., Suite 250
Washington, D.C. 20007

This association provides general information about spina bifida and resulting conditions, information concerning informal education and handicapped individuals, recreation/physical education, and prosthetics. The SBAA will answer inquiries, make referrals to direct service providers, and provide brochures and publications. Most general information is without charge.

SOCIETY FOR THE REHABILITATION OF THE FACIALLY DISFIGURED, INC.

550 First Avenue
New York, New York 10016

The major purposes of the society are to provide facilities for the treatment and assistance of individuals who are unable to afford private reconstructive surgical care; to assist in the training and education of personnel engaged in reconstructive plastic surgery; to initiate, stimulate, and encourage research in this field; and to carry on a public education program to make more people aware of the problems of facial disfigurement and the treatment methods currently available.

TEACHER EDUCATION DIVISION (TED)

The Council for Exceptional Children
1920 Association Drive
Reston, Virginia 22091

The purposes of this division within the Council for Exceptional Children are to stimulate and actively assist in the development and improvement of programs of preparation for teachers and other professional workers who serve exceptional children; to encourage and stimulate development and improvement of research relating to the understanding and service to exceptional children with special emphasis on teacher education; to establish and maintain active liaison relations with and urge support of CEC and divisions thereof and other appropriate organizations.

UNITED CEREBRAL PALSY ASSOCIATIONS, INC. (UCPA)

1522 K Street, N.W., Suite 1112
Washington, D.C. 20005

UCPA programs and services are directed toward a twofold goal: the prevention of cerebral palsy and meeting the needs of those who are affected by the condition and others who have similar service needs. To fulfill this goal, UCPA provides funds for research and the training of scientific personnel who work in the fields of prevention and treatment of cerebral palsy; acts as an advocate for the civil rights of the disabled in the areas of education, employment, independent living, access to public buildings, and public transportation; provides public education programs; and provides direct services including medical diagnosis, special education, parent counseling, and evaluation and treatment.

UNITED OSTOMY ASSOCIATION, INC. (UOA)
36 Executive Park, Suite 120
Irvine, California 92714

The UOA is dedicated to helping every ostomy patient return to normal living through mutual aid and moral support; education in proper ostomy care and management; exchange of ideas; assistance in improving ostomy equipment and supplies; advancement of knowledge of gastrointestinal diseases; cooperation with other organizations having common purposes; exhibits at medical and public meetings; and public education about ostomy.

U.S. COMMITTEE FOR UNICEF
331 East 38th Street
New York, New York 10016

As a nongovernmental, nonprofit organization, the committee exists to inform people in the United States about the needs of the developing world's children and UNICEF's efforts to meet those needs. The committee provides information on the cultural, social, and educational aspects of the lives of children in developing countries.

WESTERN LAW CENTER FOR THE HANDICAPPED
849 South Broadway, Suite M-22
Los Angeles, California 90014

The Western Law Center for the Handicapped is dedicated to advocacy for persons who, because of their disability, are discriminated against in areas such as housing, employment, health care, education, and social benefits. The center is staffed by attorneys trained and experienced in advocacy for the disabled. They supervise paralegals and provide training for lay advocates attached to consumer organizations serving the western United States.

Index

Note: Page numbers in italic type reference nontext material.